THE MIXED MEDIA "Hamburger" SYSTEM

A 7 STEP PLAN TO HELP YOU MAKE THE MOST INSANELY AWESOME MIXED MEDIA ART PROJECTS OF YOUR LIFE!

BY KAREN CAMPBELL
ARTIST

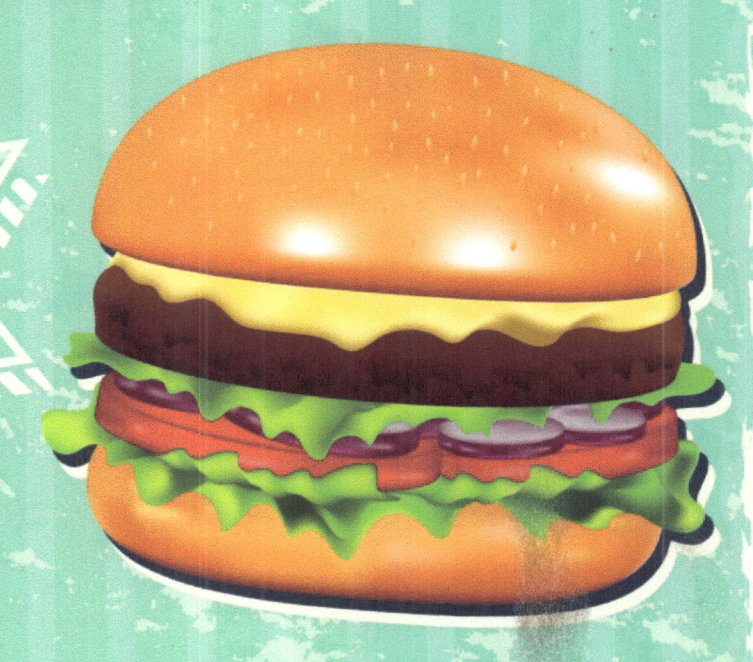

About this book

Isn't it **awesome** to sit at your art table to paint and throw a bunch of supplies around? How about stamping and stenciling your heart out? Or better yet, scribble-scrabbling on a great big canvas or a wide open art journal? It feels downright GOOD to make stuff with your own blood, sweat and tears. Right?! RIGHT.

Admit it though, deep down, a teensy weensy part of you kinda wishes that you *really truly knew* what you were doing so you'd know that whatever you were making was *guaranteed* to turn out FREAKING AMAZING.

What you need is a plan!!! Well, I made you one. It involves a hamburger (just go with it), and some steps, but it's a plan nonetheless. I think you're gonna LOVE it because it works **EVERY. SINGLE. TIME.**

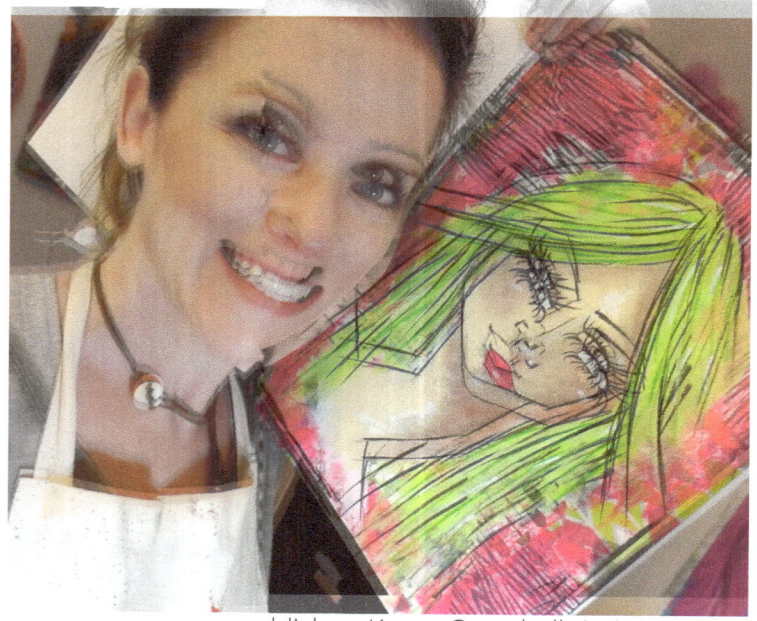

Your first job is to grasp the whole "hamburger" layering concept as a whole. You can do that by reading this book and watching the videos that go with it!

Hint: Put this URL in your browser and bookmark it!

https://bit.ly/hamburgerseries

It links to all 8 videos in the series, in order, and will get you back on track if you get lost in the cheese! Let's go make some art!

Author, Illustrator, Publisher: Karen Campbell, Artist, LLC
www.karencampbellartist.com
Book Cover Design: KT Design, LLC
www.ktdesignsllc.com
Editor: Mandi Brown

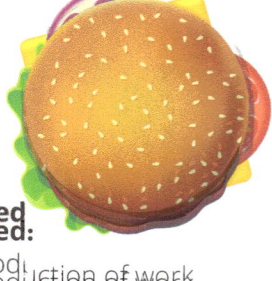

Who here is hungry besides me?!

Text and Photographs Copyright (c) 2019 by Karen Campbell. All rights reserved.

This book has been written and designed to aid the aspiring artist and hobbyist. Reproduction of work for at-home practice is permissible. Any art produced, electronically reproduced, or distributed from this publication for commercial purposes is forbidden without written content from the publisher, Karen Campbell, Artist, LLC. If you would like to use material from this book for any purpose outside of private use, prior written permission must be obtained by contacting the publisher at karen@awesomeartschool.com. Thank you for support of the author's rights.

Videos — Burger Layer — Page

Links to each individual video are on the page number listed here.

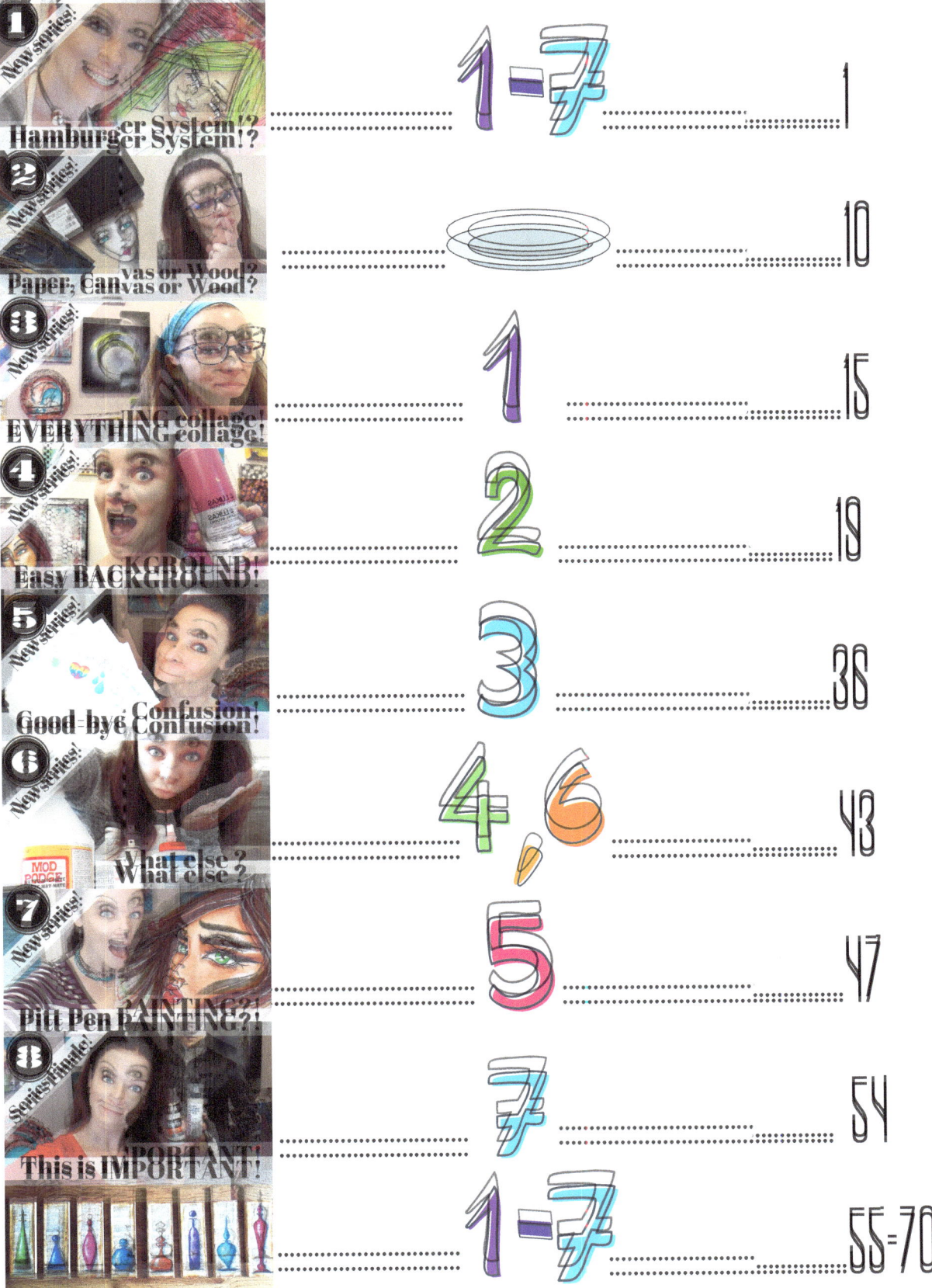

Videos	Burger Layer	Page #
1. Hamburger System!?	1-7	1
2. Paper, Canvas or Wood?		10
3. EVERYTHING collage!	1	15
4. Easy BACKGROUND!	2	19
5. Good-bye Confusion!	3	36
6. What else?	4, 6	43
7. Pitt Pen PAINTING?!	5	47
8. Series Finale! This is IMPORTANT!	7	54
	1-7	55-70

I'm assuming you bought this ridiculous sounding book because you want help in making the most insanely awesome mixed media projects?

I GOT YOU.

My name is Karen Campbell and my specialty is layering up my art supplies...

LIKE A HAMBURGER,

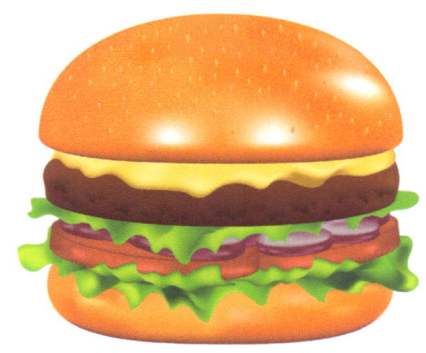

And serving them up,

AWESOME STYLE.

This guide will teach you my exact system and everything you need to know to do the same.

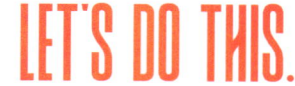

LET'S DO THIS.

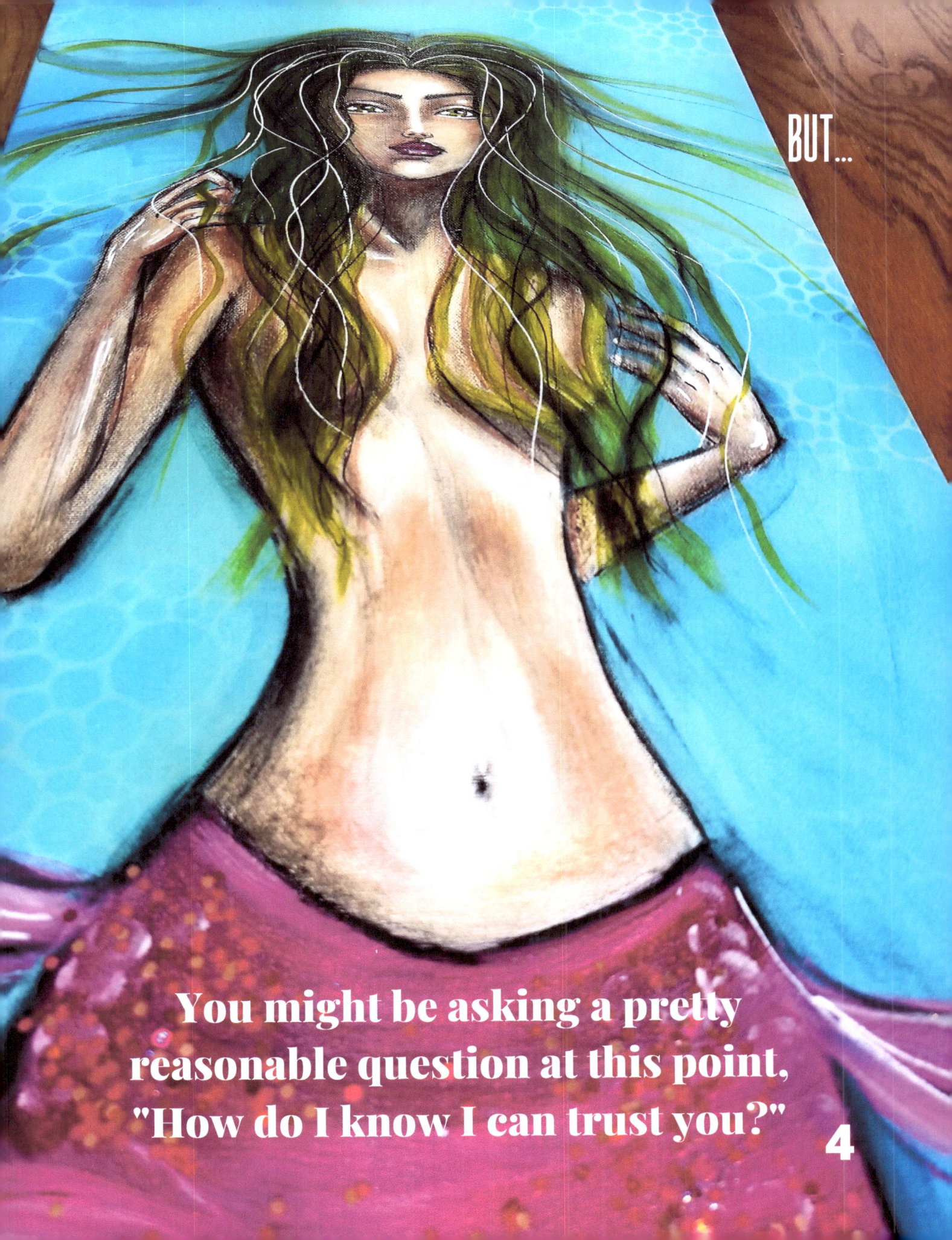

That's a fair question considering the weird, random cover of this alleged "art book".

And is perhaps due to the fact that we don't know each other quite well yet.

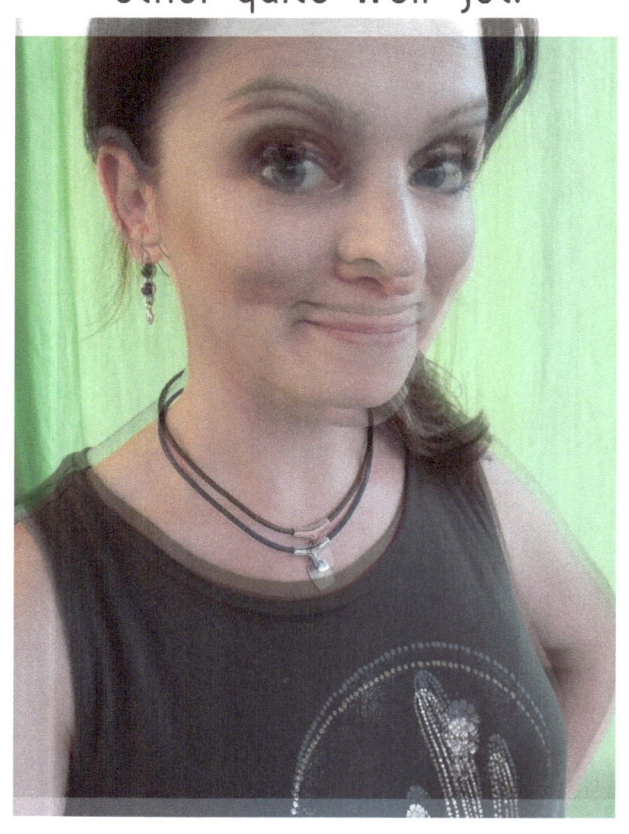

YET.

Let's just say a billion trillion completed projects couldn't be wrong.

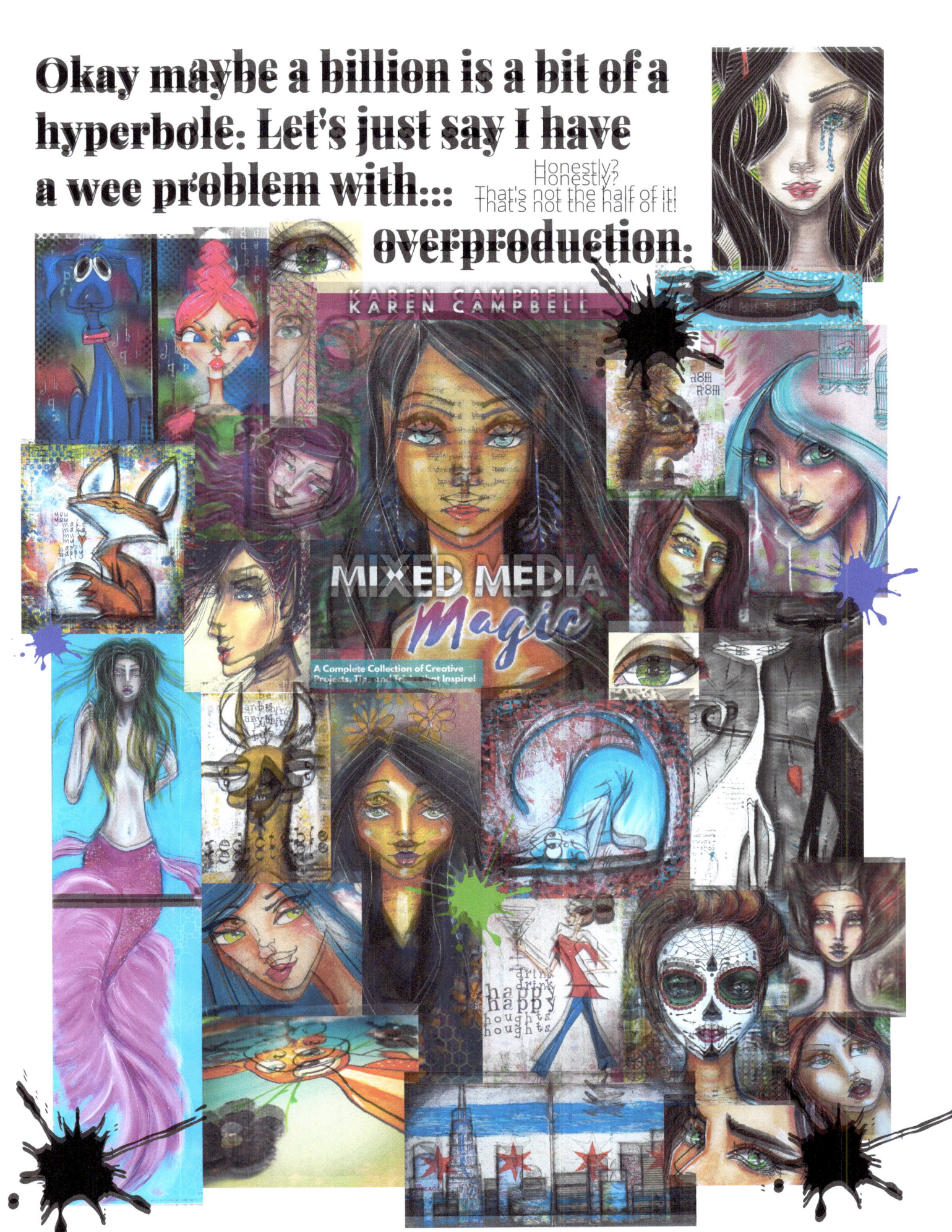

Which leads to a LOT of practice.

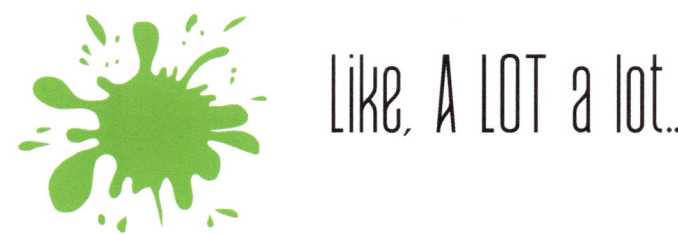

Like, A LOT a lot...

Which lead to a SYSTEM of sorts.

Which just so happened to involve a lot of layers...

Not completely unlike...

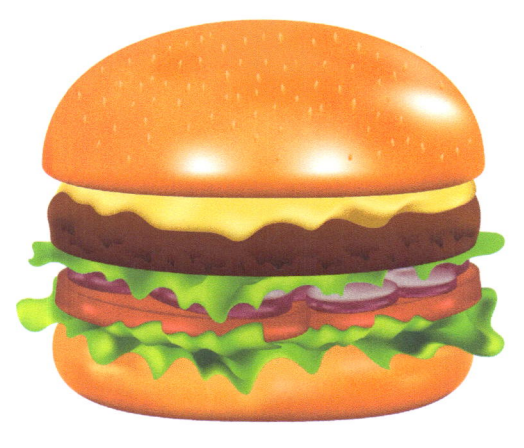

a hamburger.

You are totally diggin' this! Don't lie!

And thus, the Hamburger System was born.
Let's start with an overview.

Mixed media has a LOT of moving parts. Separating the parts into layers helps to organize our brains, our supplies, and our plan.

Check it out:

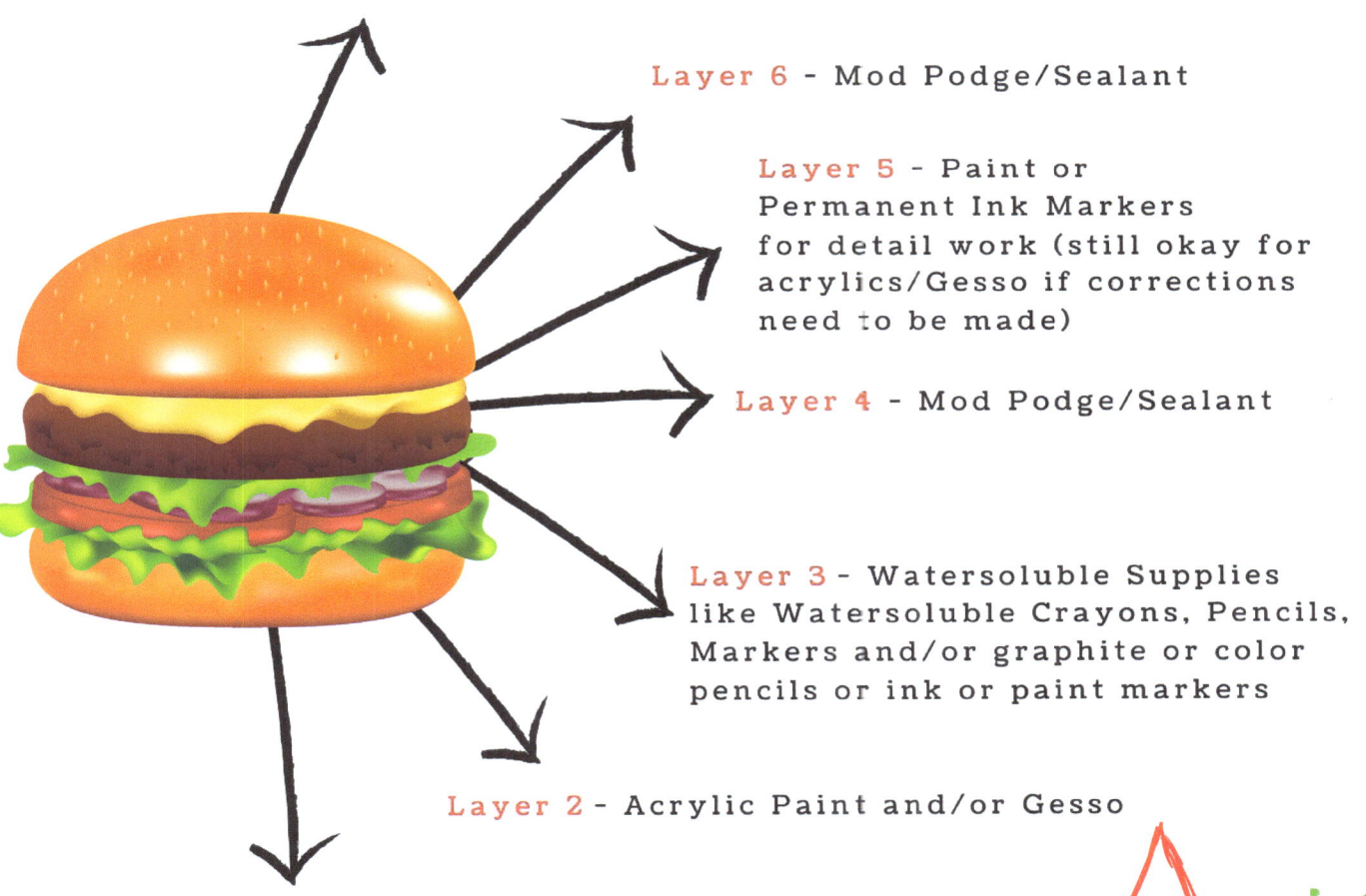

Layer 7 - Acrylic Spray Varnish/Sealant

Layer 6 - Mod Podge/Sealant

Layer 5 - Paint or Permanent Ink Markers for detail work (still okay for acrylics/Gesso if corrections need to be made)

Layer 4 - Mod Podge/Sealant

Layer 3 - Watersoluble Supplies like Watersoluble Crayons, Pencils, Markers and/or graphite or color pencils or ink or paint markers

Layer 2 - Acrylic Paint and/or Gesso

Layer 1 - Collage and Adhesive (matte medium/gel)

Build it from the bottom up

Let's take this layer by layer.
From the bottom up. ⬆
But before we build our burger,
We're gonna need a plate to put it on...

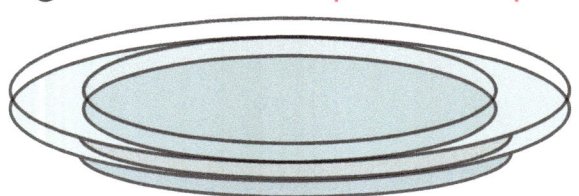

In the art world, the plate is our substrate. What are the best surfaces for making awesome mixed media projects?

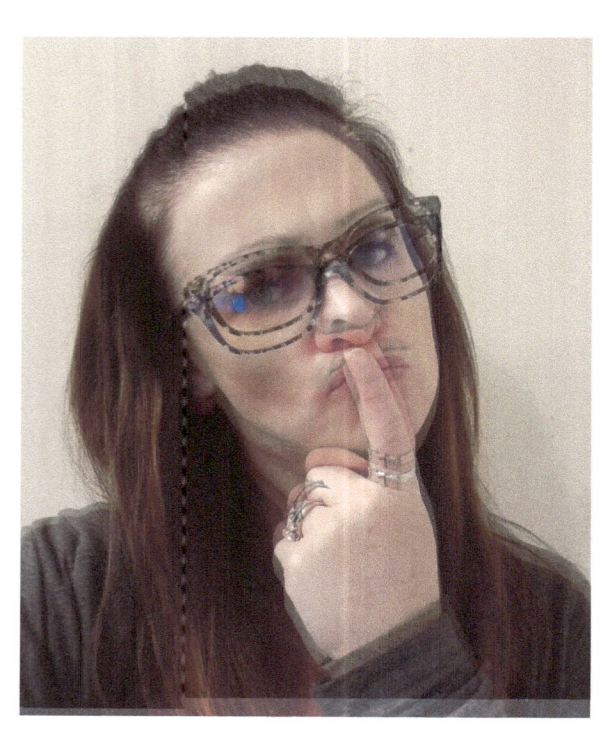

wood
canvas
art journals
canvas panels
watercolor paper
upcycled cardboard

The choices can be overwhelming!

But not if you know what to look for!

Pssst...the answer is...

watercolor paper   upcycled cardboard

wood   canvas panels

canvas   art journals

All of the above!!!

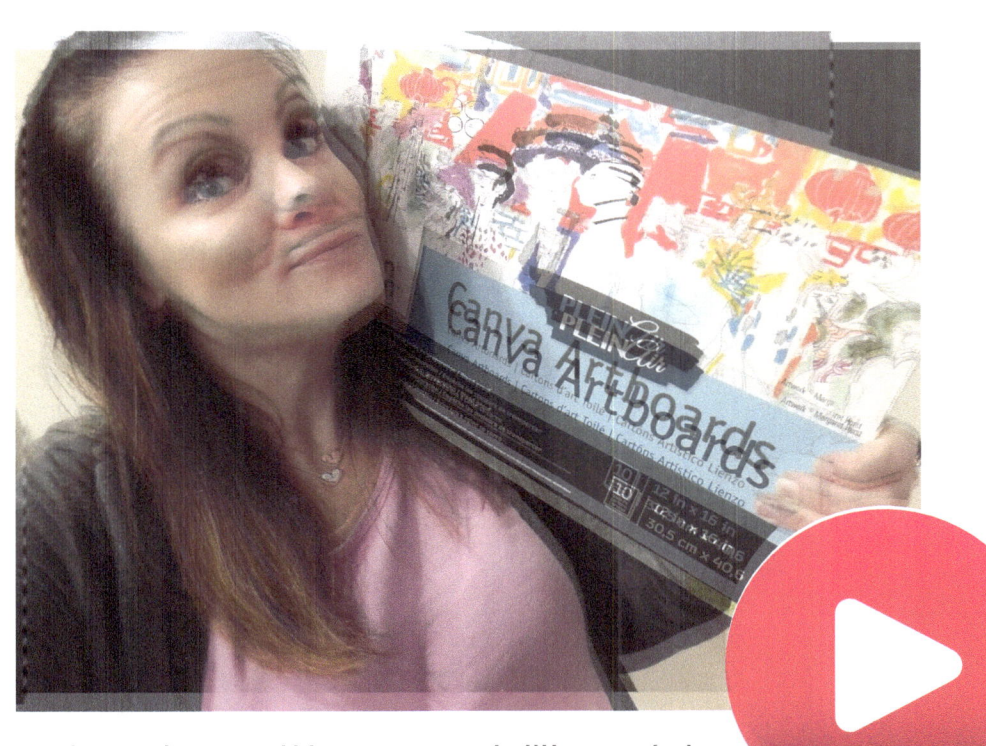

Come shopping with me and I'll explain and show you everything!   http://bit.ly/getaplate

Now that we have our plate,

we are ready for the food! The first layer is the bun.

Collage makes a GREAT BUN!

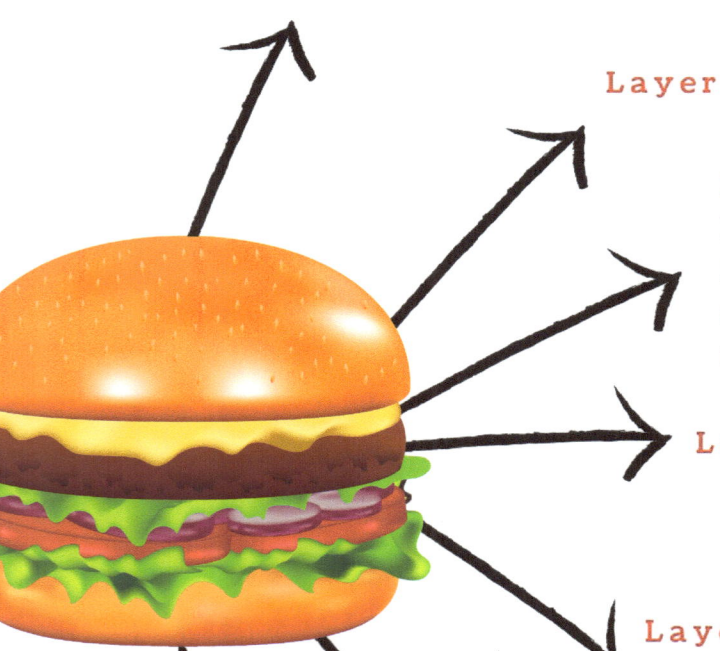

Layer 7 - Acrylic Spray Varnish/Sealant

Layer 6 - Mod Podge/Sealant

Layer 5 - Paint or Permanent Ink Markers for detail work (still okay for acrylics/Gesso if corrections need to be made)

Layer 4 - Mod Podge/Sealant

Layer 3 - Watersoluble Supplies like Watersoluble Crayons, Pencils, Markers and/or graphite or color pencils or ink or paint markers

Layer 2 - Acrylic Paint and/or Gesso

Layer 1 - Collage and Adhesive (matte medium/gel)

Let's get a move on Layer 1

Why is collage such a popular way to start mixed media projects?

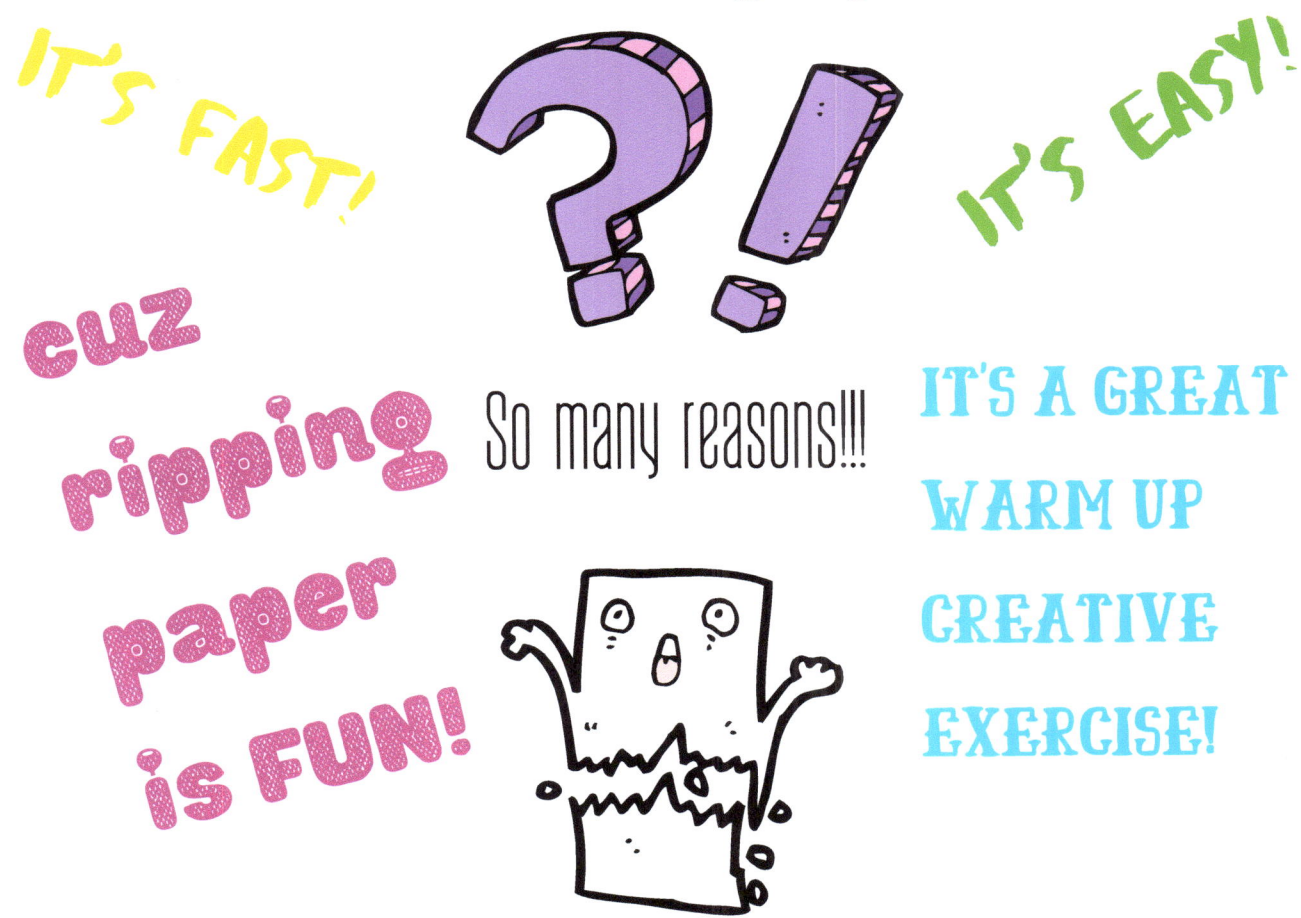

IT'S FAST!

IT'S EASY!

cuz ripping paper is FUN!

So many reasons!!!

IT'S A GREAT WARM UP CREATIVE EXERCISE!

it makes for cool texture!

it's a great way to pick the color scheme for your entire project!

literally anyone can do it!

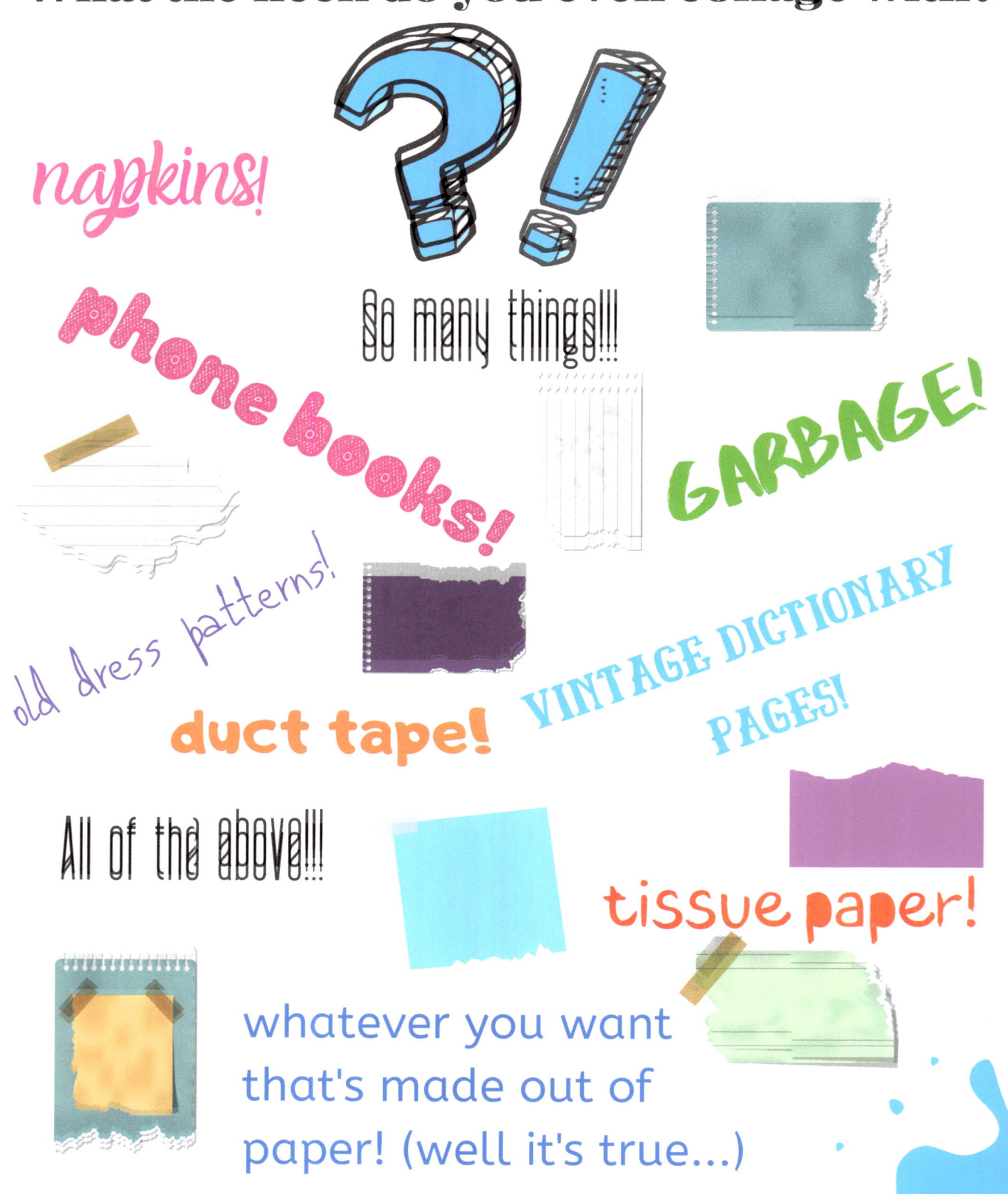

And what the heck do you glue these papers on with?

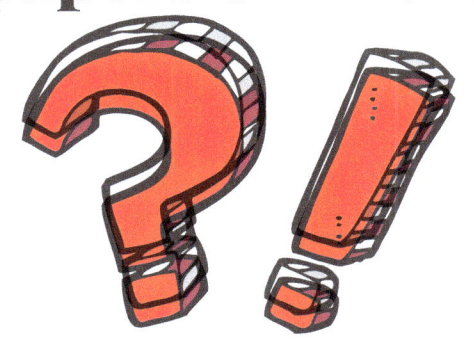

You have some choices here...

Okay Options:
Mod Podge
PVA Glue with Water
Decoupage Paste/Glue

Better Options:
Matte Medium (Liquid)
Matte Gel Medium
Soft Gel Gloss
Gloss Medium (Liquid)

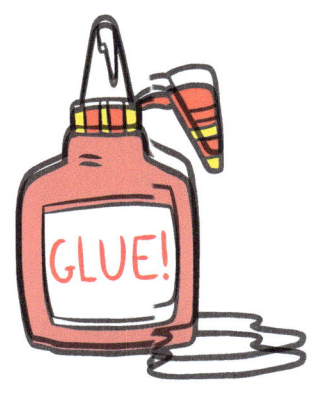
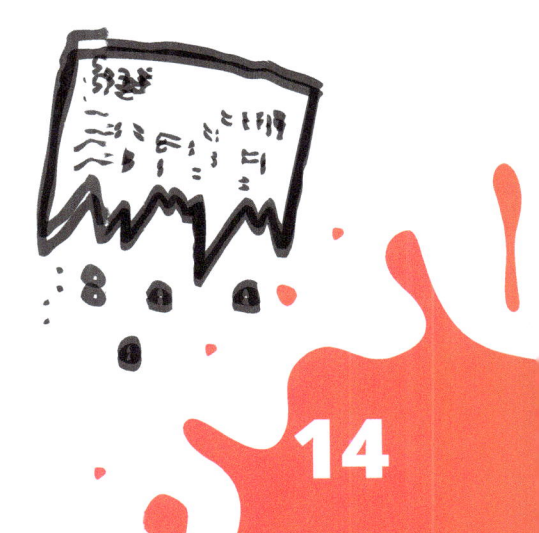

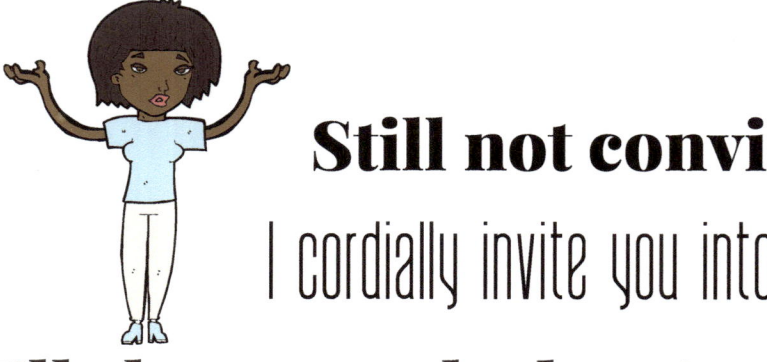 **Still not convinced?**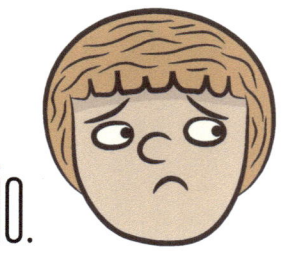
I cordially invite you into my studio.

I'll show you the how's and why's of this exciting first layer!

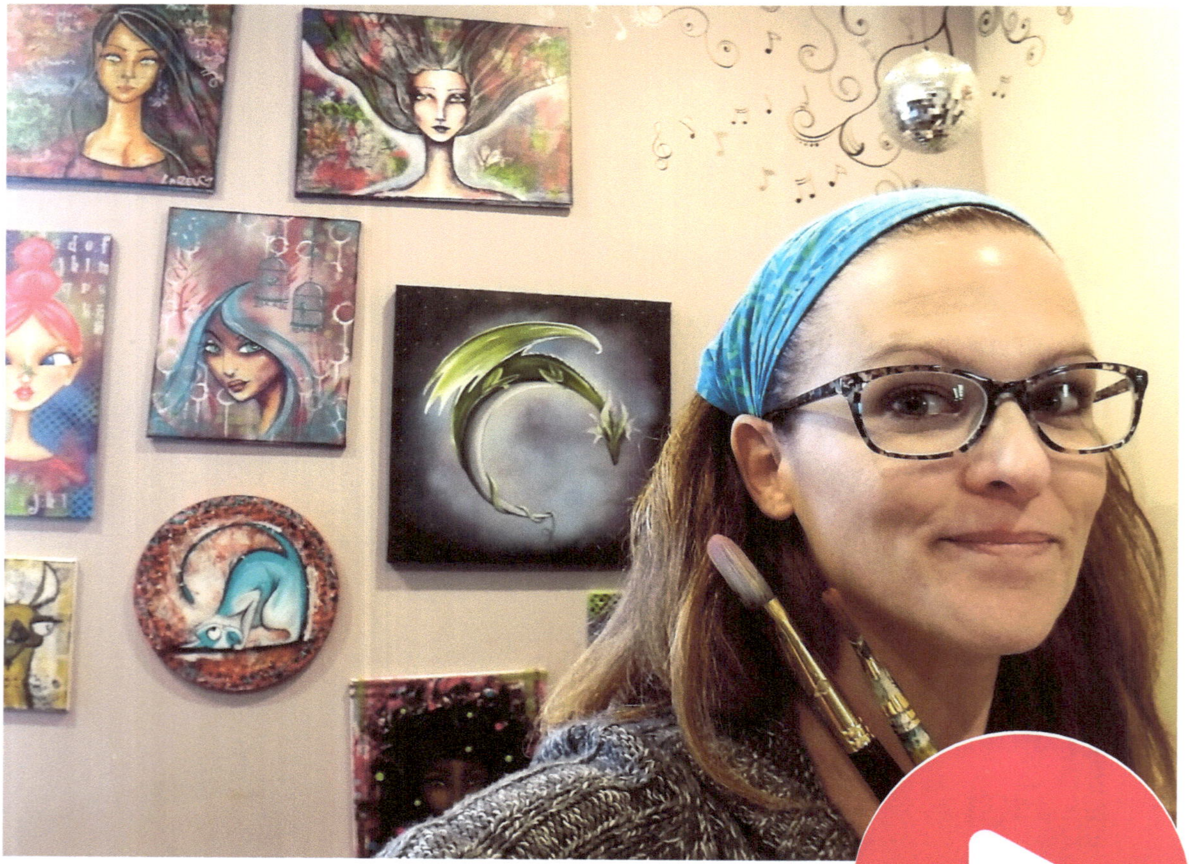

Click the link and learn all about COLLAGE!
I demo my exact process for you!

http://bit.ly/collagefirst

Woot Woot! Layer 2

Let's bust out some acrylic paints & Gesso.

It's background time, baby!

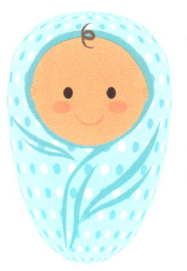 Wow, a literal baby! OMG.

Layer 7 - Acrylic Spray Varnish/Sealant

Layer 6 - Mod Podge/Sealant

Layer 5 - Paint or Permanent Ink Markers for detail work (still okay for acrylics/Gesso if corrections need to be made)

Layer 4 - Mod Podge/Sealant

Layer 3 - Watersoluble Supplies like Watersoluble Crayons, Pencils, Markers and/or graphite or color pencils or ink or paint markers

Layer 2 - Acrylic Paint and/or Gesso

Layer 1 - Collage and Adhesive (matte medium/gel)

Build it from the bottom up

Backgrounds are easy and fun!
It's play time, Layer 2!
Pick paint colors that match your collage,
and go to town! You can...

Take a credit card and SCRAPE the paint across the edges like a frame!

Use a sponge, a stencil, and some stamps!

USE A FORK TO MAKE LINES ACROSS YOUR CANVAS!

Take a brush and delicately paint lovely even strokes, changing colors as you go down your page...

Use your fingers to smear the paint in different directions and pretend that you're 6 years old!

Gesso is your best friend.

If you make a mistake, Gesso can help fix it! In so many different ways it is there to help!

Let me introduce you!

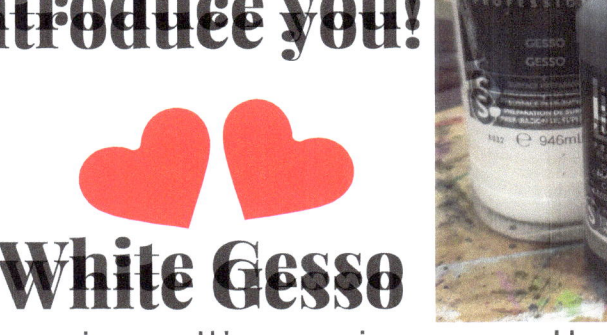

White Gesso

Is basically just a primer. It's semi-opaque. You can prep any surface for painting by putting down Gesso first, even over that awesome collage you just made.

Made a mistake? Put down Gesso and start fresh again.

Clear Gesso

Is for when you want to paint over part of an existing painting, without covering up your designs underneath!

Black Gesso

Is kind of a miracle, actually. 1000% opaque, and amazing at obliterating ugly pages you never want to see again!
Then you're free to paint something new on top!

Learn about my FAVE fun, fast and *easy* backgrounds!

I do my backgrounds for a zillion different looking pieces, all the same exact way! Gotta love the burger!

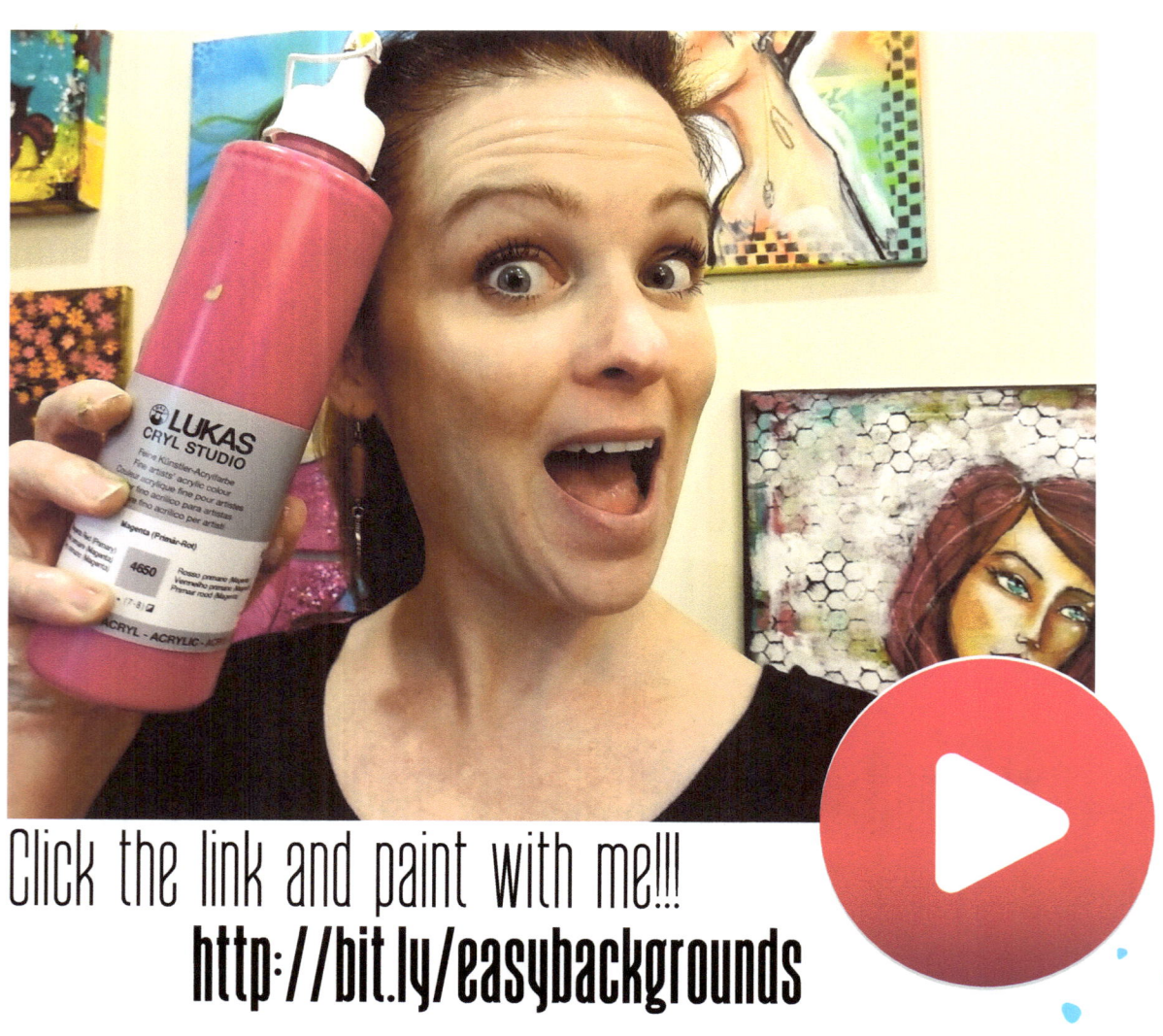

Click the link and paint with me!!!
http://bit.ly/easybackgrounds

Layer 3 is a DOOZY.

Need to serious it up, just a bit for this part!

We have our backgrounds done.

Now we need to figure out what to put on top!

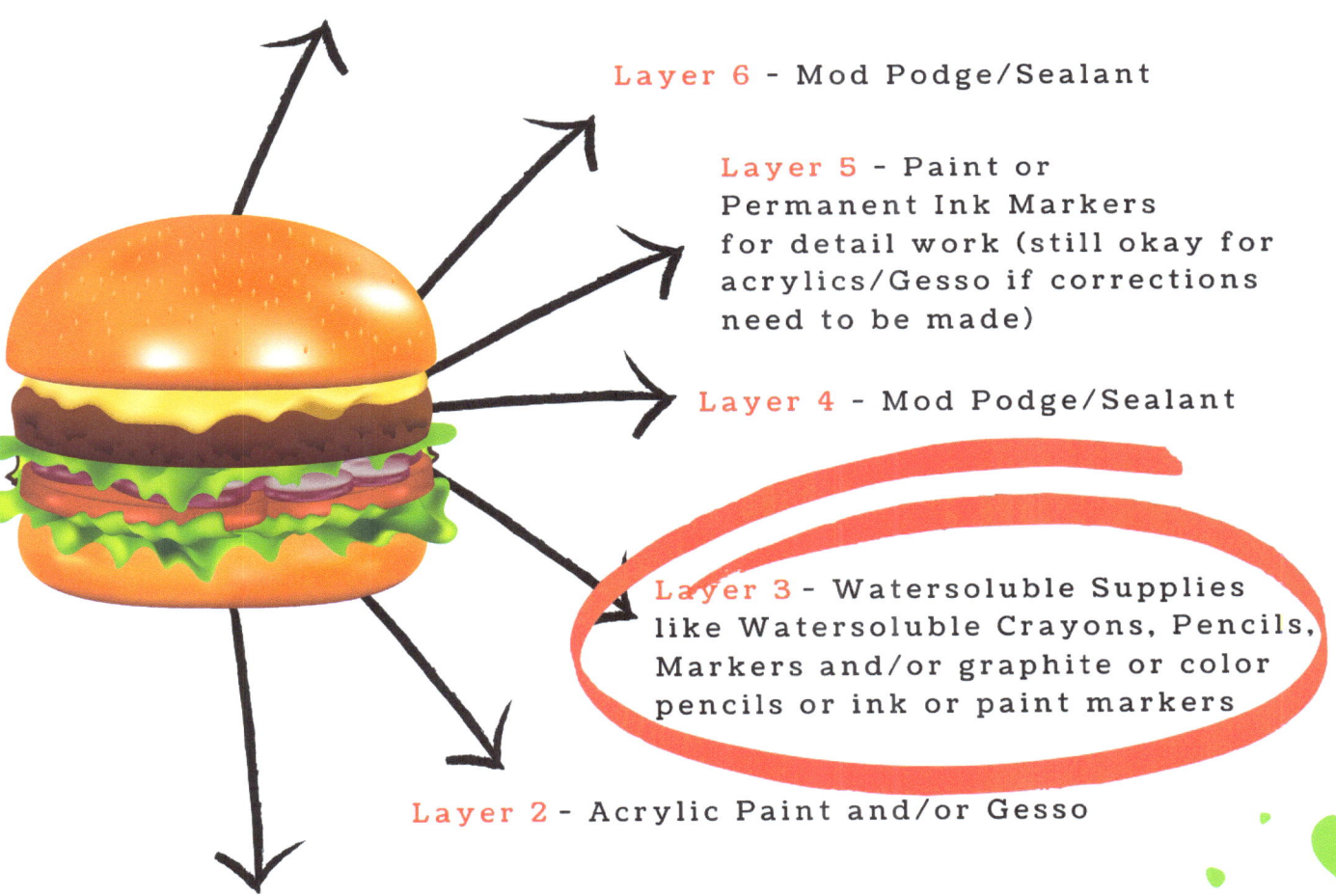

Layer 7 - Acrylic Spray Varnish/Sealant

Layer 6 - Mod Podge/Sealant

Layer 5 - Paint or Permanent Ink Markers for detail work (still okay for acrylics/Gesso if corrections need to be made)

Layer 4 - Mod Podge/Sealant

Layer 3 - Watersoluble Supplies like Watersoluble Crayons, Pencils, Markers and/or graphite or color pencils or ink or paint markers

Layer 2 - Acrylic Paint and/or Gesso

Layer 1 - Collage and Adhesive (matte medium/gel)

Here's the skinny:

You have a LOT of choices when it comes to buying art supplies.

This is the layer where we have the most options of what we can choose to use.

Whatever we choose, it has to go ON TOP of acrylic paint.

So it must be the following:

It must be Waterbased ONLY.

Yeah, okay, that's about it. Sounds simple, right?! Not so much.

There can be a lot of CONSEQUENCES when we use certain products.

Like "activating"!! And smeeeeearing!

AND - there are a ton of supplies on the market to choose from.

Too many choices can quickly become overwhelming.

First, let's figure out your priorities in terms of quality.

Do you want supplies that are Artist Grade, or Craft Grade?

Then, we need to think about how your supplies are going to behave together.

If we peek ahead to Layer 4 of the burger, you will notice it says to put down a layer of Mod Podge or Sealant.

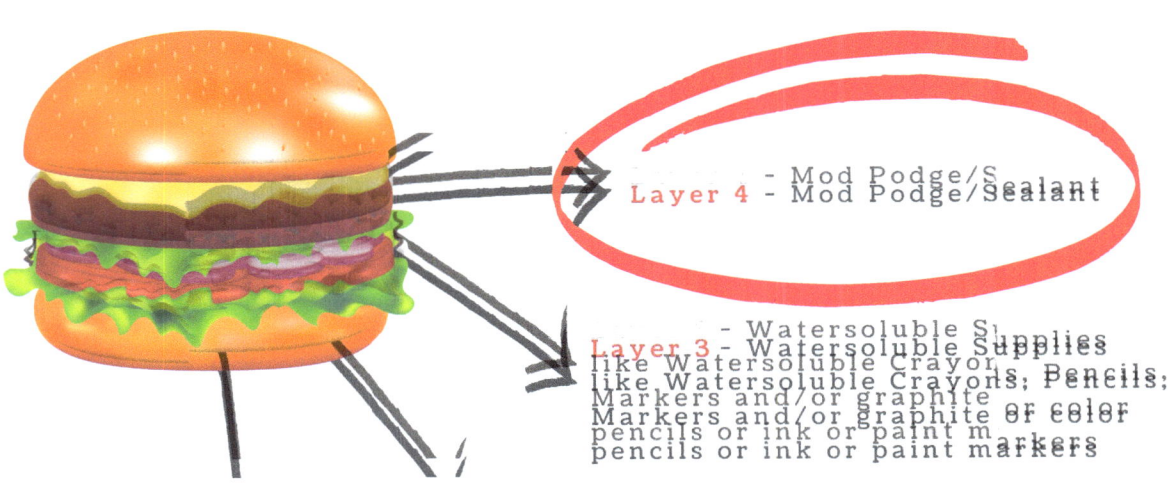

Layer 4 - Mod Podge/Sealant

Layer 3 - Watersoluble Supplies like Watersoluble Crayons, Pencils, Markers and/or graphite or color pencils or ink or paint markers

That means we need to know what the heck is going to happen to all the supplies we use in Layer 3...

WHEN THEY GET **WET**.

Ask yourself: Do I care about quality? Will I be selling or gifting my original work? Will I want it to last a long time?

IF YES, CHOOSE FROM ARTIST QULALITY BRANDS ONLY

There are a LOT of phenomenal art supply brands on the market and I can't possibly list them all here. But keep your eyes peeled for these brands and you'll be in safe hands when you're shopping in stores or online.

GOLDEN	CHARVIN	FABER-CASTELL	PENTEL
LIQUITEX		STABILO	PRISMACOLOR
LUKAS	OLD HOLLAND	DERWENT	CARAN-D'ARCHE
WINSOR- NEWTON		SENNELIER	STAEDTLER
HOLBEIN		MARABU	VAN-GOGH

What if you're in the store and are not sure about a brand?

How do you know if you've found a quality product that will work great in your burger?

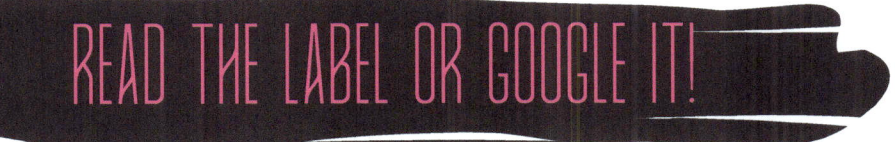 READ THE LABEL OR GOOGLE IT!

You are looking for some or a lot of these key words!

LIGHTFAST

PIGMENT-INK BASED

ARCHIVAL

ACID-FREE

PERMANENT

WAX BASED

ARTIST GRADE

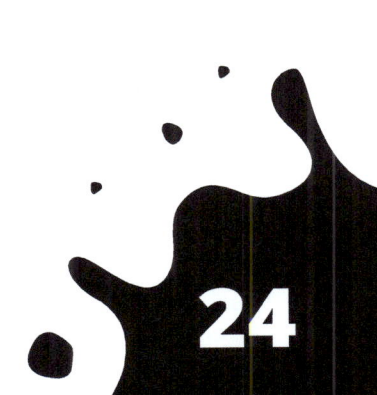

The products you can use in layer 3 are varied and FUN! These are some of my favorite artist grade supplies!

GELATOS BY FABER-CASTELL
They are not only **watersoluble & lightfast**, but also odorless and best of all, permanent when dry. (fabercastell.com)

PITT PENS BY FABER-CASTELL
Unlike other art pens or markers which are alcohol and dye-based, Pitt Artist Pens are 100% India ink. They are non-toxic and odorless. The ink is **lightfast and permanent** when fully dry on porous surfaces. They are extremely fade-resistant, archival, acid-free, smudge proof and waterproof when dry. (fabercastell.com) And, they come in an insane amount of colors!

PENTEL POCKET BRUSH PEN
Featuring rich black, **permanent pigmented (lightfast) ink** and a flexible fiber brush tip, this pen is perfect for making any mark ranging from fine details to sweeping strokes — all from one pen! Best tool for eyelashes!

STABILO ALL PENCILS
Stabilo's soft, waxy leads mark on virtually any surface. Use them for writing in color on paper and other surfaces (even difficult surfaces like plastic, film, and mylar). Available in 8 colors. (Dickblick.com)

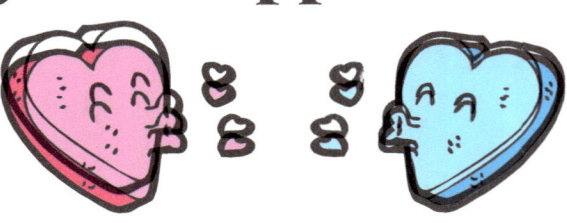

ART CRAYONS BY MARABU
Lightfast & buttery smooth, **richly pigmented** wax based pastel and comes in 25 colors. Watersoluble.

UNI-POSCA PAINT PENS
Water-based **pigment ink** is **lightfast and water-resistant** and writes on virtually any surface - yet does not bleed through paper. The wide range of opaque colours cover each other well.

BOMBAY INKS BY DR. PH MARTIN
The Bombay inks are **pigment based india inks, acid-free, archival grade, lightfast, waterproof & non-toxic**.

NOODLER'S INKS
These come in 2 varieties: Bulletproof (ie. permanent) and Extremely Water-reactive. Their colors are to die for! Read the fine print before buying so you know which colors react how!!

Here are some other fun, fine grade products to play with in Layer 3

PANPASTELS

Only professional artists' grade pigments are used for the most concentrated colors possible. The colors have **excellent lightfastness** and are fully erasable.

PRISMACOLOR ILLUSTRATION MARKERS

These markers contain premium pigmented **acid-free, archival ink that is lightfast, permanent, non-toxic**, and water resistant. (DickBlick.com)

CARAN D'ACHE LUMINANCE ARTIST PENCILS

Caran d'Ache wax based pencils with excellent **lightfastness** (non-watersoluble).

DERWENT - INKTENSE PRODUCTS

100% of colours within the Inktense Paint Pan Set are lightfast, meaning the pigment will remain **chemically stable** under long exposure to light. 90% of colours within the Inktense Pencils and Inktense Blocks ranges are lightfast. (Derwent.com)

CARAN D'ACHE SUPRACOLOR PENCILS & NEO COLOR II'S

Caran d'Ache colored pencils and crayons lay down color really well, and blend beautifully. Available in 76 **extremely lightfast** colors, they are 100% watersoluble and very highly pigmented.

THIS LIST CAN BE WAAAAAY BIGGER!

Use the next page to add on to this list. Write it YOUR favorite artist grade options!

26

My favorite, awesome artist quality products:

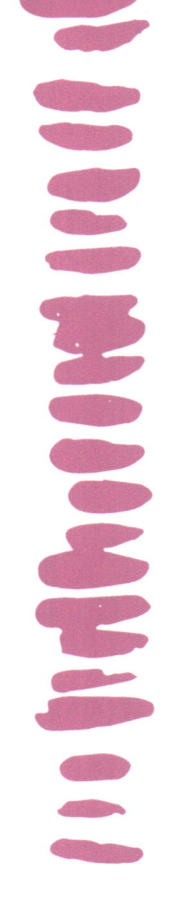

BRAND NAME:

Type (Paint, Marker, Pencil, etc):

Favorite Colors:

Where I purchased:

BRAND NAME:

Type (Paint, Marker, Pencil, etc):

Favorite Colors:

Where I purchased:

BRAND NAME:

Type (Paint, Marker, Pencil, etc):

Favorite Colors:

Where I purchased:

BRAND NAME:

Type (Paint, Marker, Pencil, etc):

Favorite Colors:

Where I purchased:

Because Mixed Media is a messy affair with paint and glue...
We need to understand what happens to the marks our products make when they get WET...

IF YOU WANT A TON OF SMEARING, CHOOSE FROM THIS CATEGORY

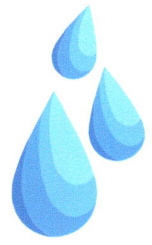 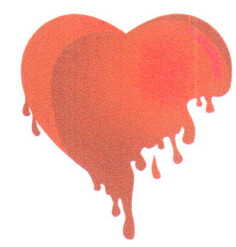

IF ONLY A LITTLE BLENDING IS DESIRED, CHOOSE FROM THIS CATEGORY

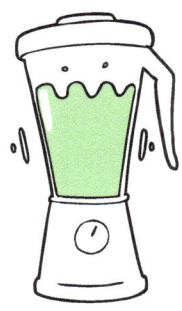

IF NO MOVEMENT IS DESIRED, CHOOSE FROM THIS CATEGORY

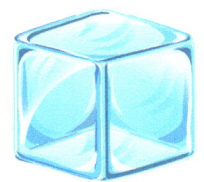

Favorite Artist Grade Products & How they react to liquid (water, paint, etc)

EXTREME ACTIVATION
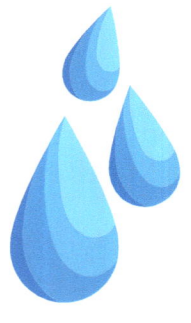

MODERATE MELT

LOVELY BLEND
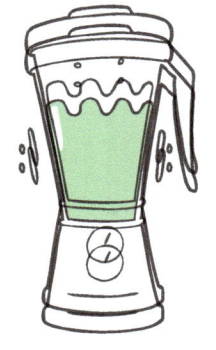

FROZEN = NOT GOING ANYWHERE
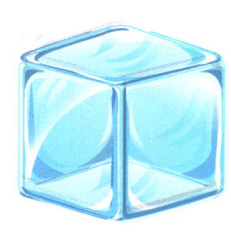

- Stabilo All Pencils
- Winsor-Newton Watercolor markers (way harder to use on acrylics, can be okay if mixed with gesso or activated with gesso to move around over the acrylic layer)
- Watersoluble Inks (read your labels!!)
- Graphitone Pencils by Derwent

- Watercolor pencils
- Inktense products
- USA General's Black watercolor pencil (great alternative to the Stabilo All because not as reactive, but you still get a nice jet-black)

- Gelatos by Faber-Castel
- Art Crayons by Marabu
- Graphite Pencils
- PanPastels (not positive!)

- Pitt Pens
- Uni-Posca Paint Pens
- Paint Markers filled with acrylic paint/ink
- India Ink Products
- Acrylic Paints & Inks
- Prismacolor Lightfast Woodcase Colored Pencils
- Caran D'arche Luminance Pencils
- Pentel Pocket Brush Pen

Feel free to add your own favorites to this list!

29

How do you tell how your art products will react to liquid?
TEST 'EM OUT!

1) Grab a paint brush and some water.
2) Run some water over your test scribble.
3) See how much your art supply moves!

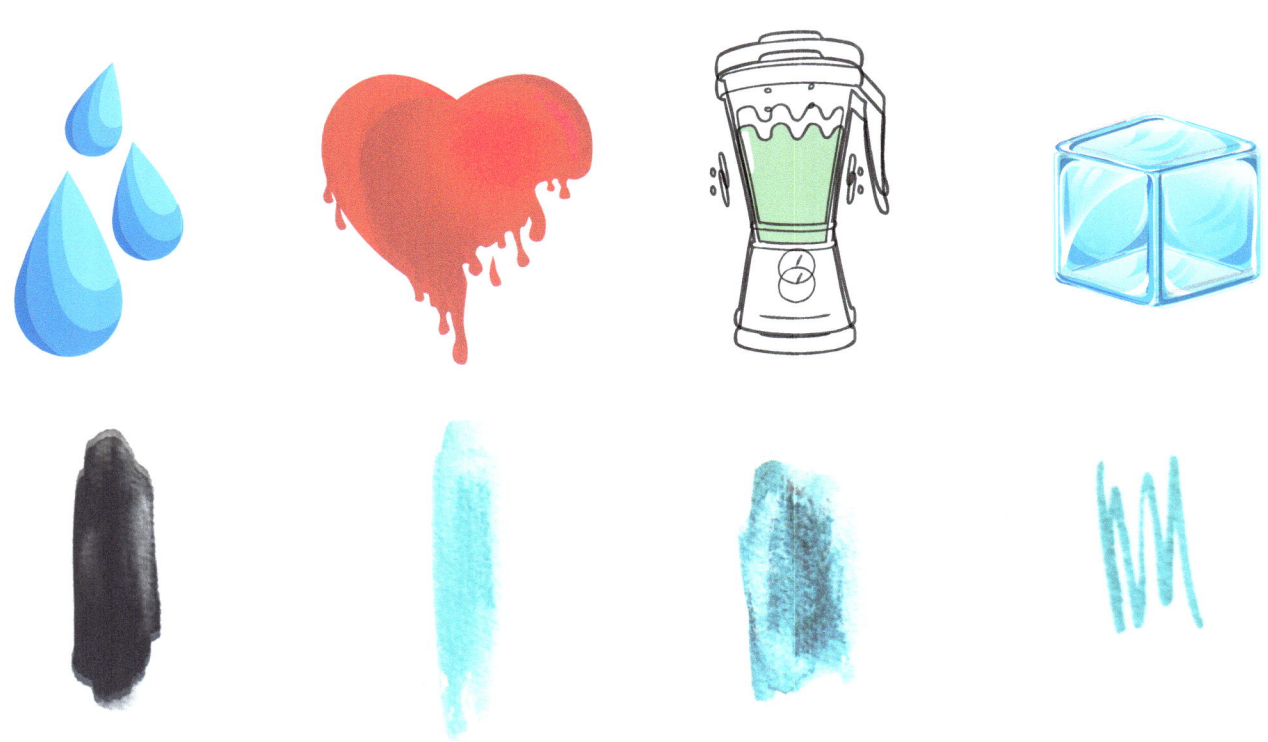

This is my Stabilo All pencil with water. See how crazy melted that is? So into this category it goes!

This is a Caran D'arche watercolor pencil. See how it is totally activated but you can still see some of the pencil marks left behind?

This is an Art Crayon by Marabu. Lots more left behind on this one, right? A lovely blend indeed!

This is a Uni-Posca Pen! 100% acrylic paint in here so it ain't movin!

If you're creating for yourself and longevity of your piece isn't of importance, you can save a LOT of money *and* have a BLAST by using craft grade products!

JUST BE FOREWARNED: MOST ARE NOT LIGHTFAST!

There are a LOT of super fun craft supply brands on the market and I can't possibly list them all here. Keep your eyes peeled for these brands, and you're sure to have fun with these products next time you sit down at your art journal or easel!

RANGER	RECOLLECTIONS	CRAYOLA
ECOLINE	NICOLE	DYLUSIONS
JANE DAVENPORT	BRUSHO	TIM HOLTZ

Fun Craft-Grade Products

Waterbased & blendable supplies that play well with others!

EXTREME ACTIVATION

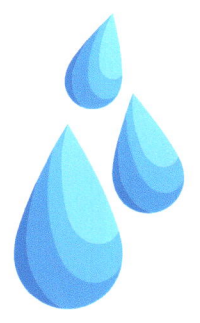

MODERATE MELT

LOVELY BLEND

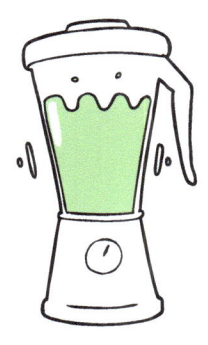

FROZEN - NOT GOING ANYWHERE

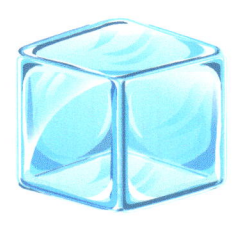

- Dylusion Sprays
- Tombow Markers
- Ecoline Watercolors and Brush markers
- Brusho's Powder

- Ecoline Markers
- Distress Inks
- Distress Markers
- Distress Stains
- Elegant Writer Calligraphy Pen

- Distress Crayons
- Super soft graphite pencils

- Craft Paint Acrylic
- Inks (permanent, Indian)

Here are some of my favorite brands!

TOMBOWS

These are one of my fave products for ease of use and blendability. Dual Brush Pens are ideal for artists and crafters. The **water-based ink is blendable** and the resilient nylon brush retains its point stroke after stroke (Tombowusa.com) They come in almost 100 colors! What's not to love?!

JANE DAVENPORT PRODUCTS

Many fun colors and products to choose from!

ECOLINE PRODUCTS

Dye based watercolor and brush pens in lovely colors that are **highly reactive**!

DYLUSION PRODUCTS

So fun! But also so fading so be forewarned!

TIM HOLTZ'S DISTRESS INK PRODUCT LINE

Tim Holtz Distress® Inks are a collection of acid-free, non-toxic, fade resistant, water-based dye inks. BUT because they are dye based, they do fade, and quite a bit.

BRUSHO'S

Colourcraft claims that Brusho will hold up over time, but being dyebased, Brusho is not lightfast nor archival.

PRISMACOLOR PENCILS

There are only a few colors that test well for lightfastness, that's why this brand is in the craft category and not the previous one. Surprising! I know! You can research these by color to find out the specific ratings of each one if you want to know more.

ELEGANT WRITER BY SPEEDBALL

Made with crisp, chisel nibs and free-flowing, acid-free ink that **changes colors when wet**! Black can dissolve into blues, greens and even subtle pinks and purples! Dye based so will fade.

JUST BE AWARE:

Just like for Artist Grade products, it's impossible for me to list all the brands that are great. Remember most (but not all) craft grade products ARE *NOT* LIGHTFAST, which means that they contain ingredients and/or properties that may fade or fail over time.

EDUCATE YOURSELF by reading labels or Googling product names if you are unsure!

My favorite, awesome craft grade supplies:

BRAND NAME:

Type (Paint, Marker, Pencil, etc):

Favorite Colors:

Where I purchased:

BRAND NAME:

Type (Paint, Marker, Pencil, etc):

Favorite Colors:

Where I purchased:

BRAND NAME:

Type (Paint, Marker, Pencil, etc):

Favorite Colors:

Where I purchased:

BRAND NAME:

Type (Paint, Marker, Pencil, etc):

Favorite Colors:

Where I purchased:

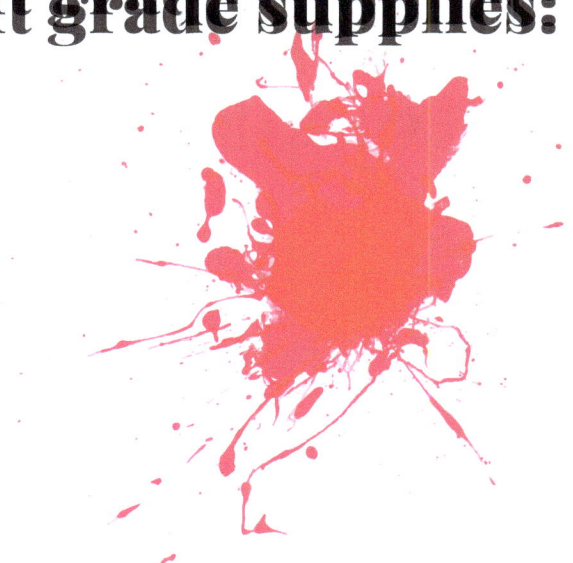
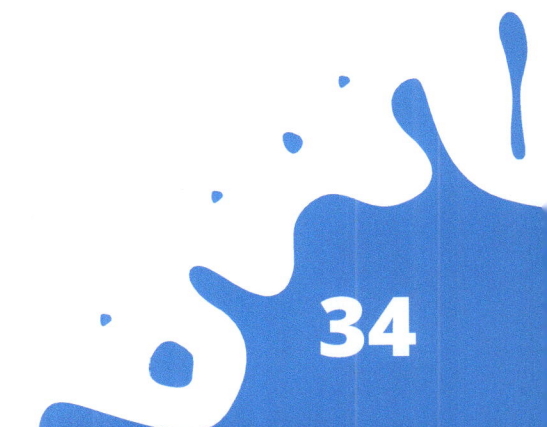

I want your mixed media pieces to be super successful! Avoid the following supplies in your hamburger layers...

COPICS OR SHARPIES & OTHER ALCOHOL BASED PRODUCTS

But why?

Copics and alcohol markers are SO MUCH FUN! They are great for illustration, card making and art journaling. Because they are alcohol based, they fade/discolor over time and don't layer over **or** under layers of acrylic paint well and may be easily damaged by mixed media work. They also aren't opaque, which is another reason why trying to layer them over acrylics is...well, somewhat futile!

OIL BASED PRODUCTS

But why?

For so many reasons. Because they can take months to dry. Because while you can layer them over acrylics, they fight for dominance when paired with or under other acrylic or water-based products. If an oil product is going to be your very, very *final* layer, on top of acrylics and everything else you've got going on in your project, then you're fine. But then you're not building a Hamburger anymore. That's more of a Reuben. Which is also totally fine, just not what we are focusing on in this video series!

STRAIGHT-UP WATERCOLORS

But why?

The main reason is that in layer 2 of the Hamburger System we are painting with Acrylics. When acrylic paints dry, they essentially become a solid, non-porous, plastic surface. Watercolors need a porous surface in order to not just simply slide right off your page! Can you add a layer of watercolor ground or gesso and then watercolor on top of that? The answer is sure! But then you're building a slider and this particular system, my friends, is just the Hamburger. We will be getting into other systems down the road, so subscribe to my YouTube channel before you forget, and stay tuned to learn more!

There's a LOT in these pages!
If you're a visual person (and if you own this book then you are!)

You will appreciate the full demo of it all in action!
I highly recommend watching this video here:

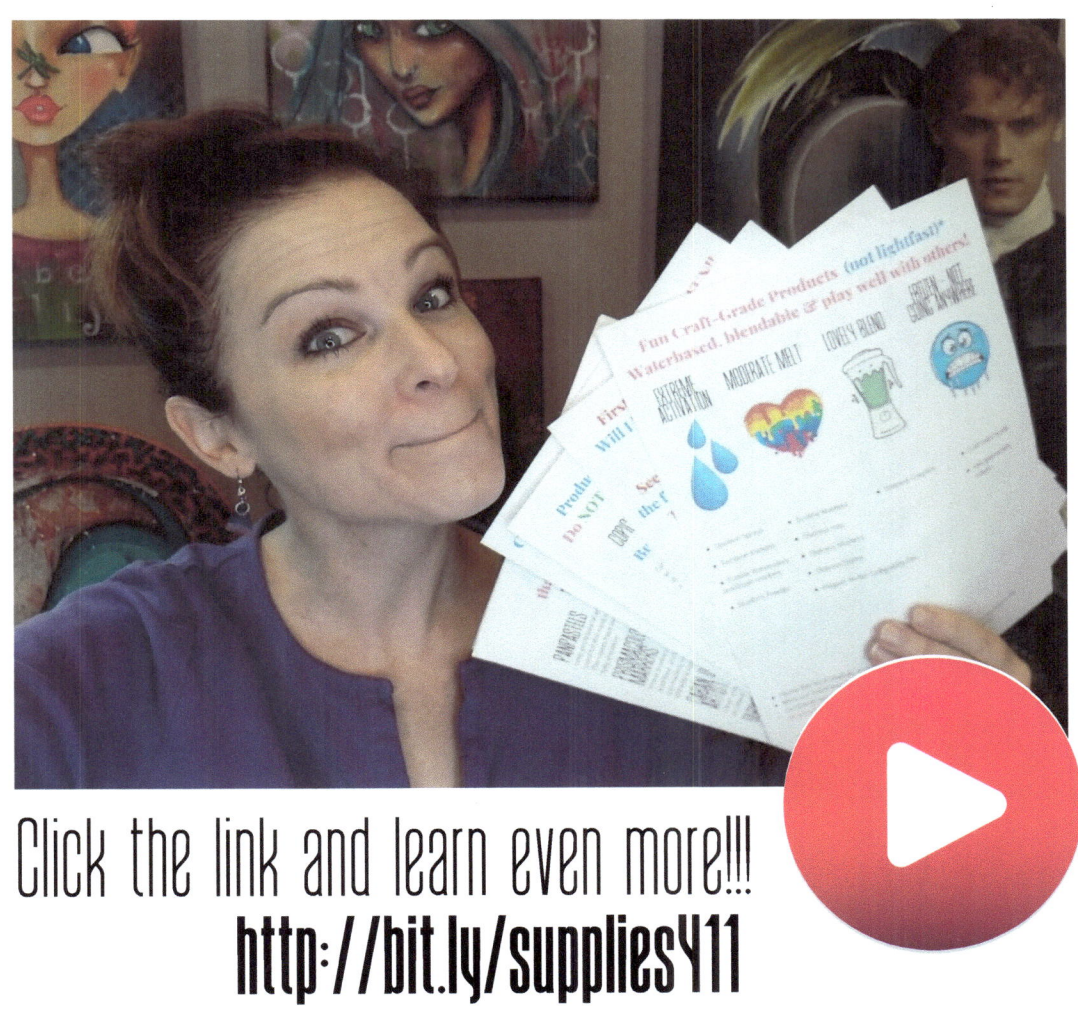

Click the link and learn even more!!!
http://bit.ly/supplies411

Psst...those papers in my hand? Those are the starting papers of this booklet so don't worry about getting them, they're already yours!

To seal or not to seal?
That is the question!

A question we will come across 3 separate times (or more!) in the Hamburger system...

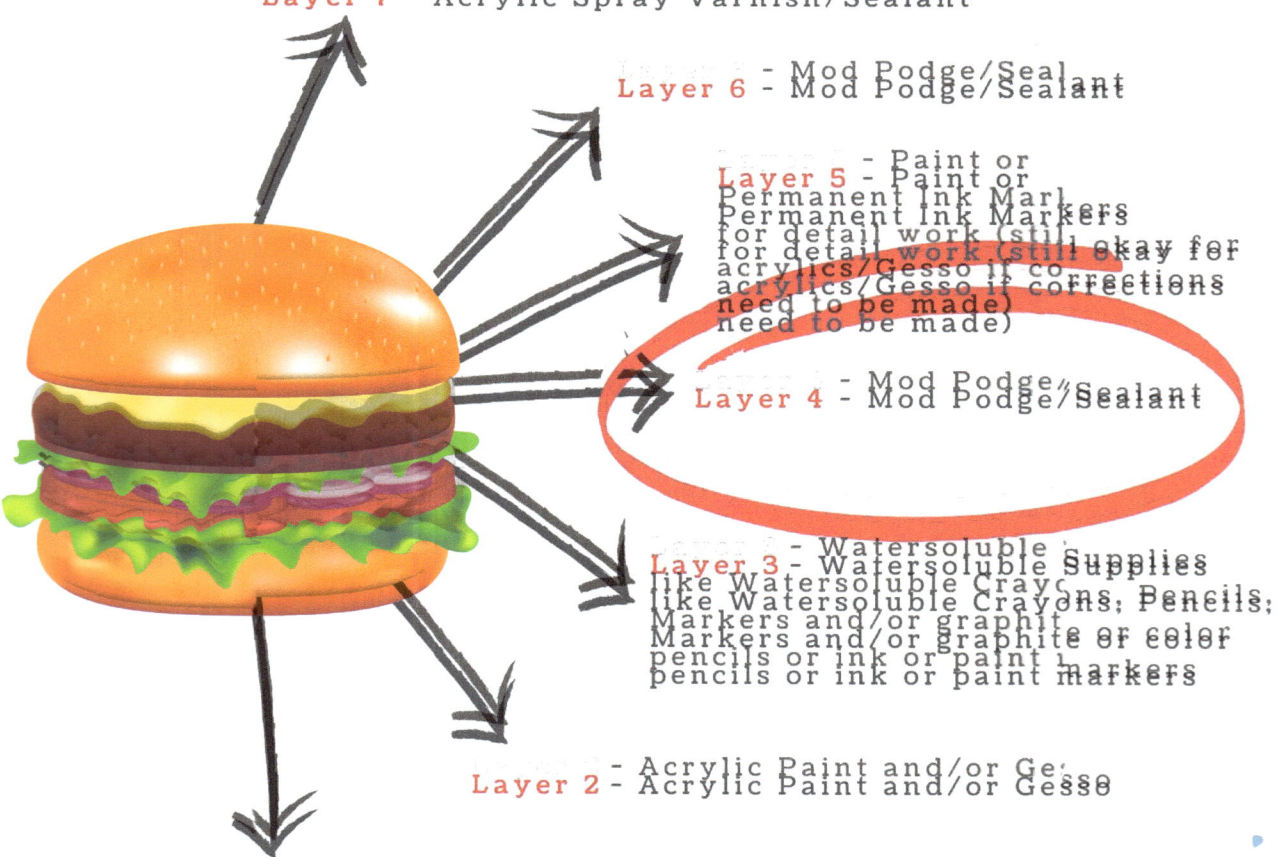

Layer 7 - Acrylic Spray Varnish/Sealant

Layer 6 - Mod Podge/Sealant

Layer 5 - Paint or Permanent Ink Markers for detail work (still okay for acrylics/Gesso if corrections need to be made)

Layer 4 - Mod Podge/Sealant

Layer 3 - Watersoluble Supplies like Watersoluble Crayons, Pencils, Markers and/or graphite or color pencils or ink or paint markers

Layer 2 - Acrylic Paint and/or Gesso

Layer 1 - Collage and Adhesive (matte medium/gel)

Build it from the bottom up

To recap our burger thus far...

On the plate we have collage papers and glue

Then we added acrylic paint & gesso...

Followed by some drawing stuff.

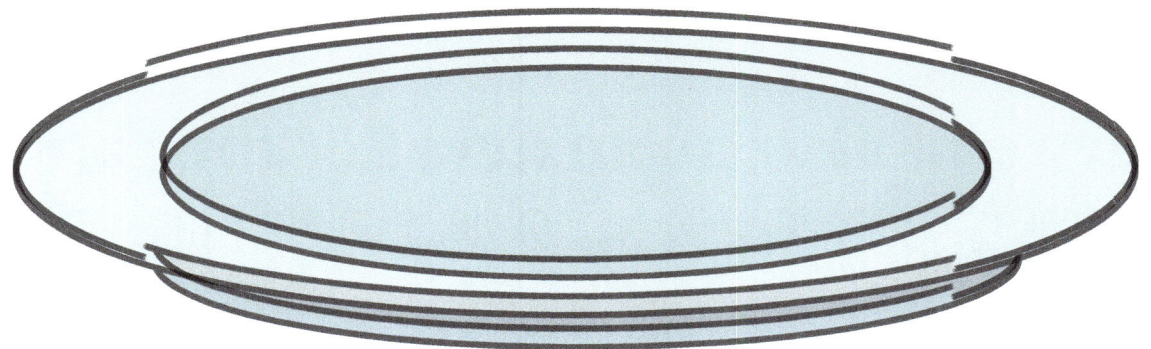

This is a good time to seal all the layers so far.

But once again, we have a few choices, so buckle up.

Commencing Layer 4...

We need a sealer, or sealant
to "lock down" our previous layers of collage, painting and drawing!

Sealers *can* come in the form of a glue.
But, they don't have to.

They *do have to* dry CRYSTAL CLEAR,
so we don't cover up our work thus far!

A sealer can also be an acrylic "medium,"
a clear or white substance (either liquid or gel) that can be mixed into acrylic paint to change its properties.

Often times, acrylic mediums *also* have great adhesive qualities!
Think fancy glue, that you can mix in with your paints!

That's why when you use these glues and mediums, they make such great sealants!
They are literally gluing down all your work!

Sealer FAQ's

1) Are all sealers glue?

Not necessarily. But for the Hamburger method we want them to be!

2) Can you use sealers for a final layer?

Yes and No. It depends on the product. Read your labels, they will tell you. Most acrylics mediums were NOT meant to be the final layer, it'll say so right on the bottle!

3) Which products CAN double as a sealer and final layer?

From the list below (which are the ones that I've personally tested) only *Mod Podge* or *Gloss Medium & Varnish* are suitable for the final layer.

However **if you are working in an art journal, you should not use Mod Podge as the final layer as your pages will stick together when closed.** Instead, make sure you spray or coat your pages with an acrylic spray sealer/finisher. See next chapter!

Use a **foam brush** for this layer as it can be really gloppy and gloopy!

Although ... all options are **100% clear** when dry!

Craft-Grade Options include:

Mod Podge

Decoupage Glue

Watered Down PVC Glue

Artist-Grade Options include:

Matte Medium

Gloss Medium

Soft Gel Medium (Gloss)

Gloss Medium & Varnish

Isolation Coat by Golden

Weldbond Universal Adhesive

After having experimented with these products, suffice to say, I imagine that most acrylic mediums can work for this layer in the hamburger, especially if they are glossy or semi-glossy!

There's one last thing...
It is not enough that this layer of sealer is looking down everything else underneath.

Oh no...
It is of equal importance that the sealant itself is smooth!!!

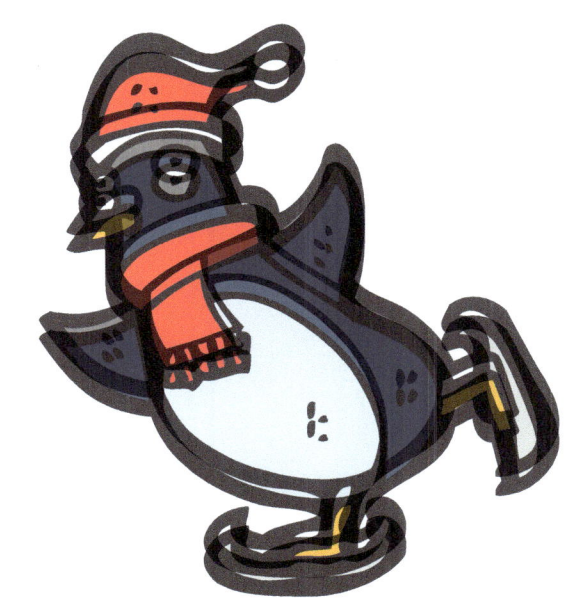

Like a skating rink!!!
Because we will be using that "smooth factor" to help us paint the next layer!

Turn to the next chapter and I'll explain!

Still confused about what sealer (and why) to apply to your hamburger?! I got you!

See me demo all 7 products, learn what they can do, & the pros and cons of each!

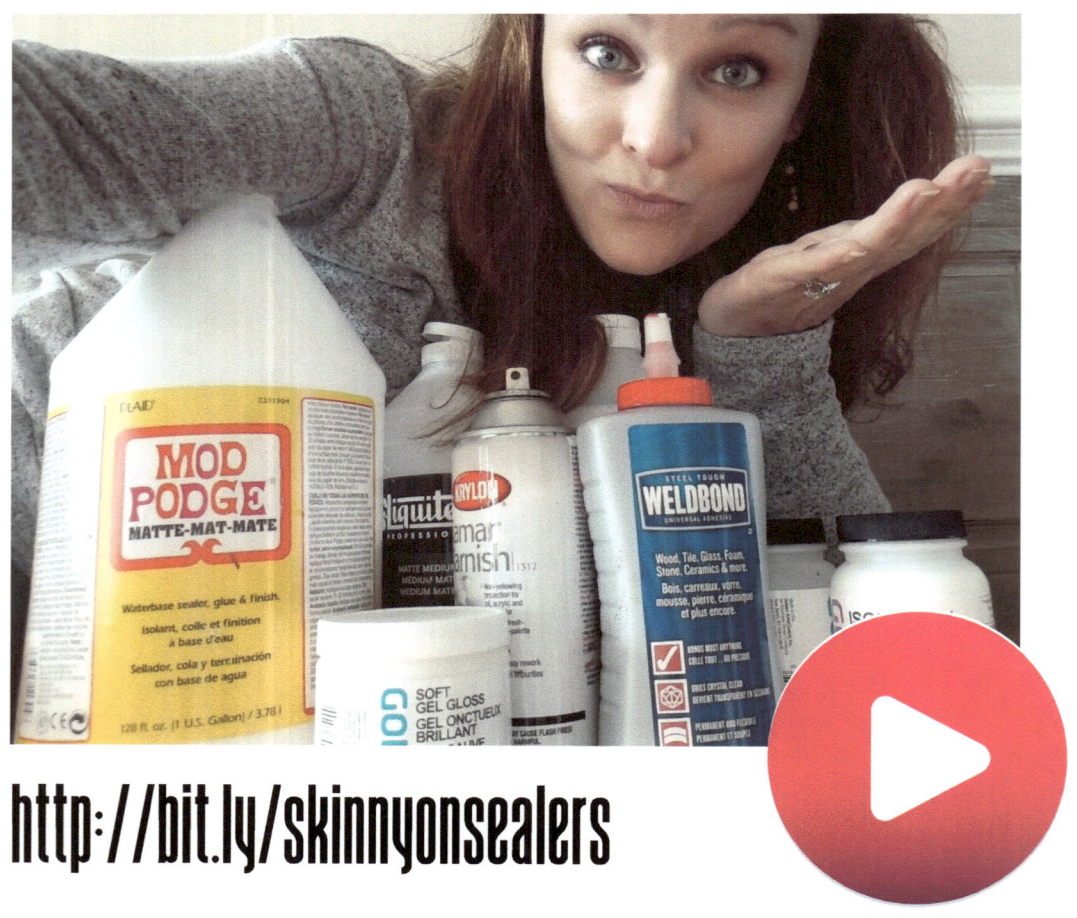

http://bit.ly/skinnyonsealers

Aren't you excited that YOU didn't have to buy all these products yourself to learn what they do?! You can thank my sweet, generous Patrons for that! You can become a Patreon Member too and get crazy awesome perks! Just visit **www.patreon.com/karencampbellartist** to learn more about giving and receiving with Patreon.

Now that all the layers are lovingly sealed up, it's time to doodle on top!

Get ready to rock Layer 5

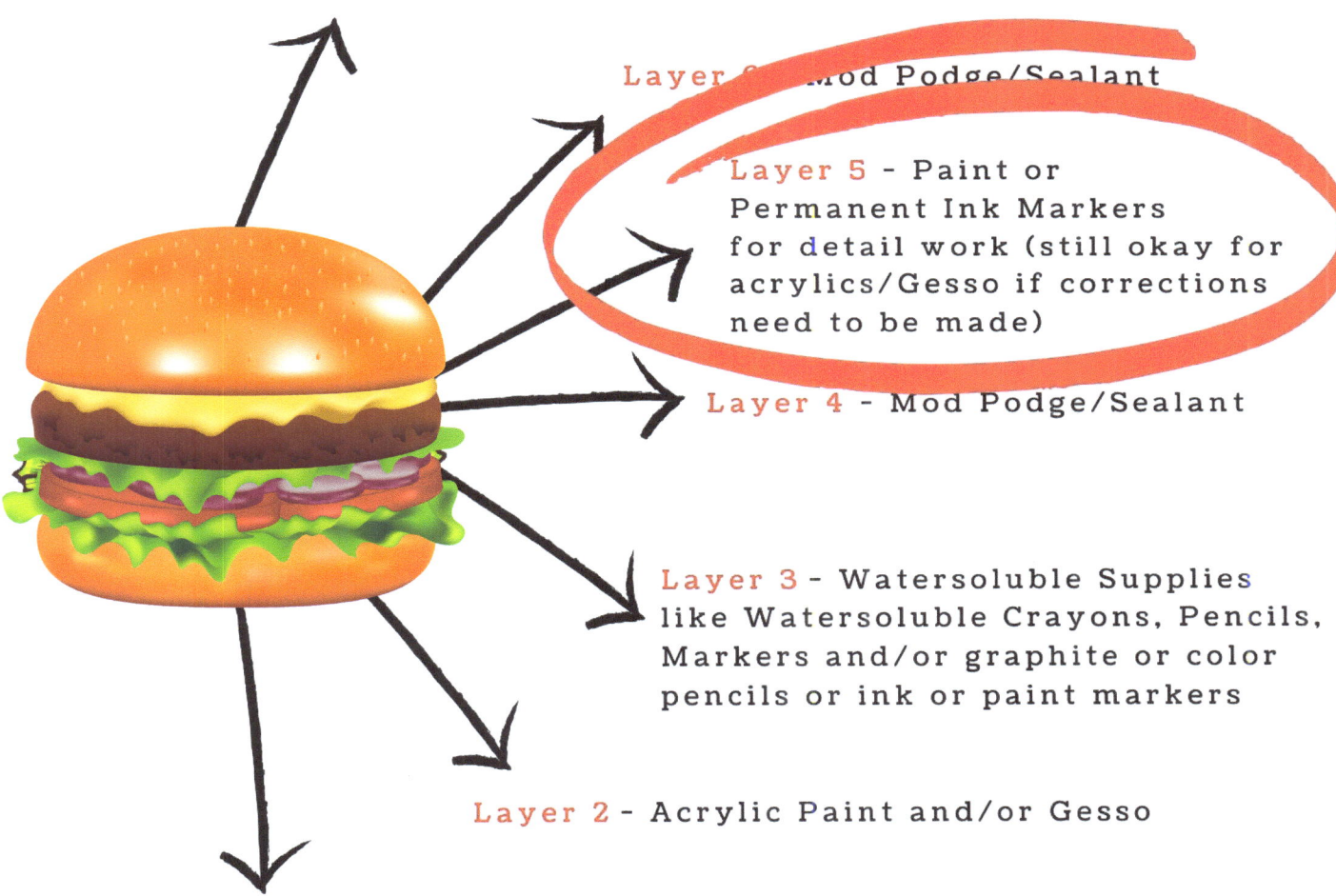

Layer 7 – Acrylic Spray Varnish/Sealant

Layer 6 – Mod Podge/Sealant

Layer 5 – Paint or Permanent Ink Markers for detail work (still okay for acrylics/Gesso if corrections need to be made)

Layer 4 – Mod Podge/Sealant

Layer 3 – Watersoluble Supplies like Watersoluble Crayons, Pencils, Markers and/or graphite or color pencils or ink or paint markers

Layer 2 – Acrylic Paint and/or Gesso

Layer 1 – Collage and Adhesive (matte medium/gel)

Build it from the bottom up

While you totally can still paint and use acrylics in Layer 5, I like to take things in a different direction!

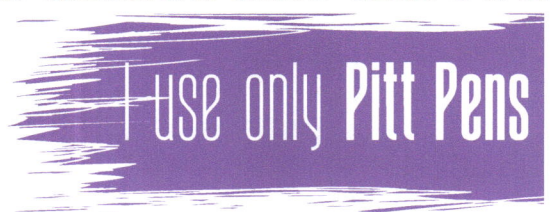

I use only Pitt Pens

I'll refresh your memory from the previous chapter about what these puppies are: "Unlike other art pens or markers which are alcohol and dye-based, Pitt Artist Pens are 100% India ink. They are non-toxic and odorless. The ink is lightfast and permanent when fully dry on porous surfaces. They are extremely fade-resistant, archival, acid-free, smudge proof and waterproof when dry." (fabercastell.com) **And come in an insane amount of colors!**

And then I make a little magic with them!

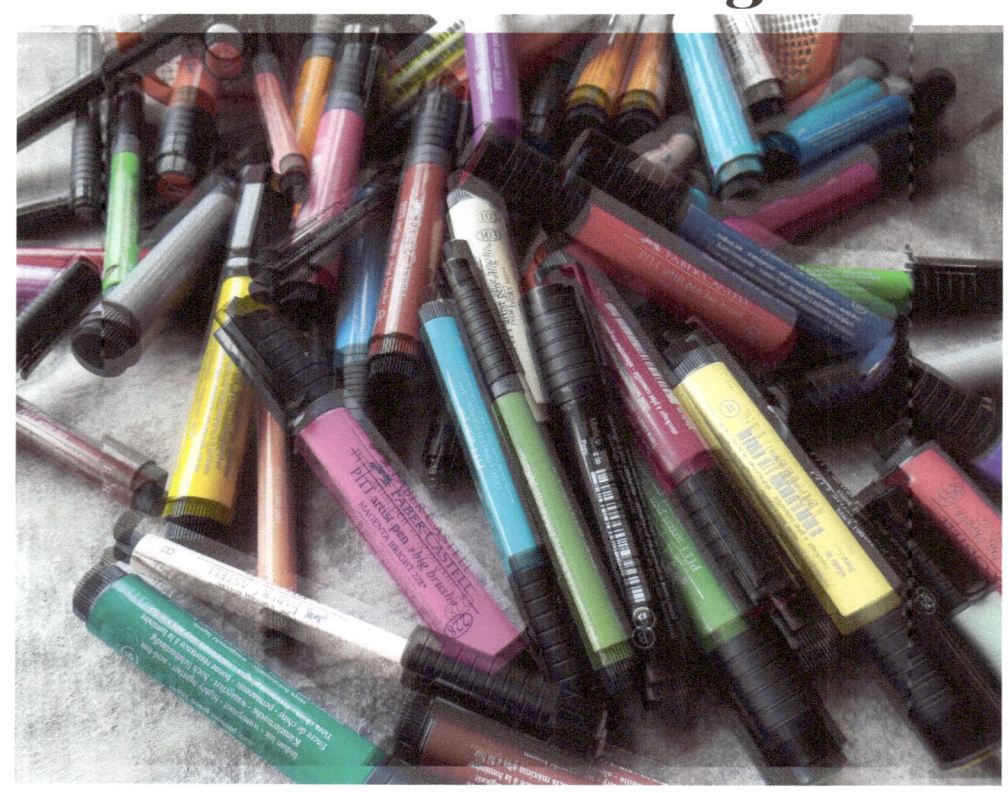

They look innocent enough, don't they?

And yes, this is a photo of my actual stash and no, I'm not sponsored (although sweet executives from Faber-Castell if you're reading this... I am TOTALLY down with that idea, just sayin)!

The magic part is this...

Because my surfaces are now nice and shiny and smooooth...

From the glossy, lovely Layer 4

I pick out Pitt Pen colors that match my acrylic paints underneath and

I start to color with the lovely brush nib.

Then, I take my finger... and simply blend the pigment.

It's literally finger painting at this point!

And shading becomes...
A veritable BREEZE!!!!
So does adding highlights for that matter!!

Because the white is so beautifully opaque!

You literally have to see this in action.
You simply won't believe it till you see it!
And just like that.
You're almost done!

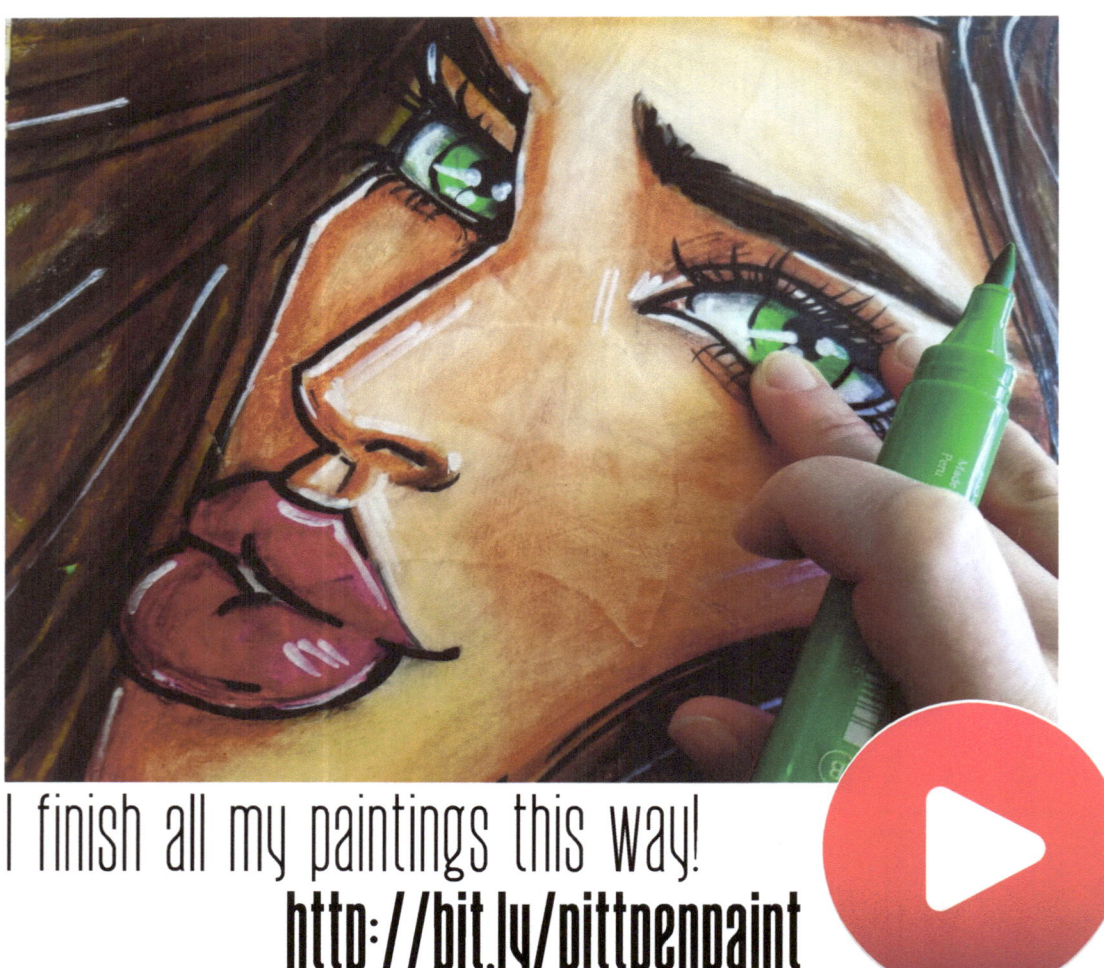

I finish all my paintings this way!
http://bit.ly/pittpenpaint

I am sure there are other artist-grade pigment ink pens on the market that would do an equally beautiful job with this! I do know that Uni-Posca Pens work great for this layer as well. As far as other options, I just have such a giant collection of Pitt Pens and they work so extraordinarily well that I haven't gathered the funds to splurge on other brands just yet! If you know of a favorite, please drop a comment in this YouTube video and let me know! I want to know, and would love to hear from you!

You can always pop in an extra layer of sealer if you want.

Essentially, you can always repeat Layer  as many times as you wish!

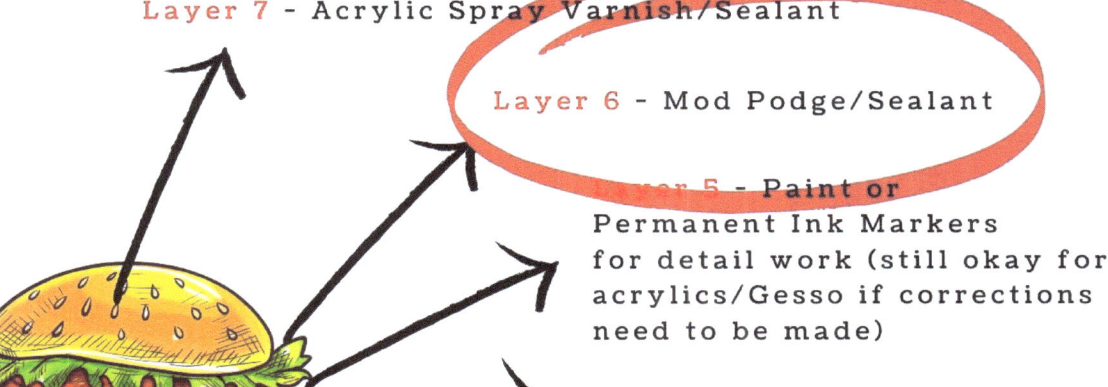

Layer 7 - Acrylic Spray Varnish/Sealant

Layer 6 - Mod Podge/Sealant

Layer 5 - Paint or Permanent Ink Markers for detail work (still okay for acrylics/Gesso if corrections need to be made)

Layer 4 - Mod Podge/Sealant

Sealer will always "refreeze" all work up to that point *completely.* Then you can repeat Layer 5 for more details and/or highlights and shading if you want to!

Or you can continue on to the last layer, Layer 7

And notice you don't go straight from layer 5 to 7. That last layer of sealant, which is Layer 6, is very important...turn the page to learn why!

48

We finally made it to the last layer!
Layer 7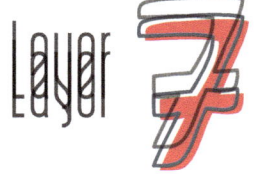

This layer (the upper bun, if you will) is
EXTREMELY IMPORTANT!
So pay attention!

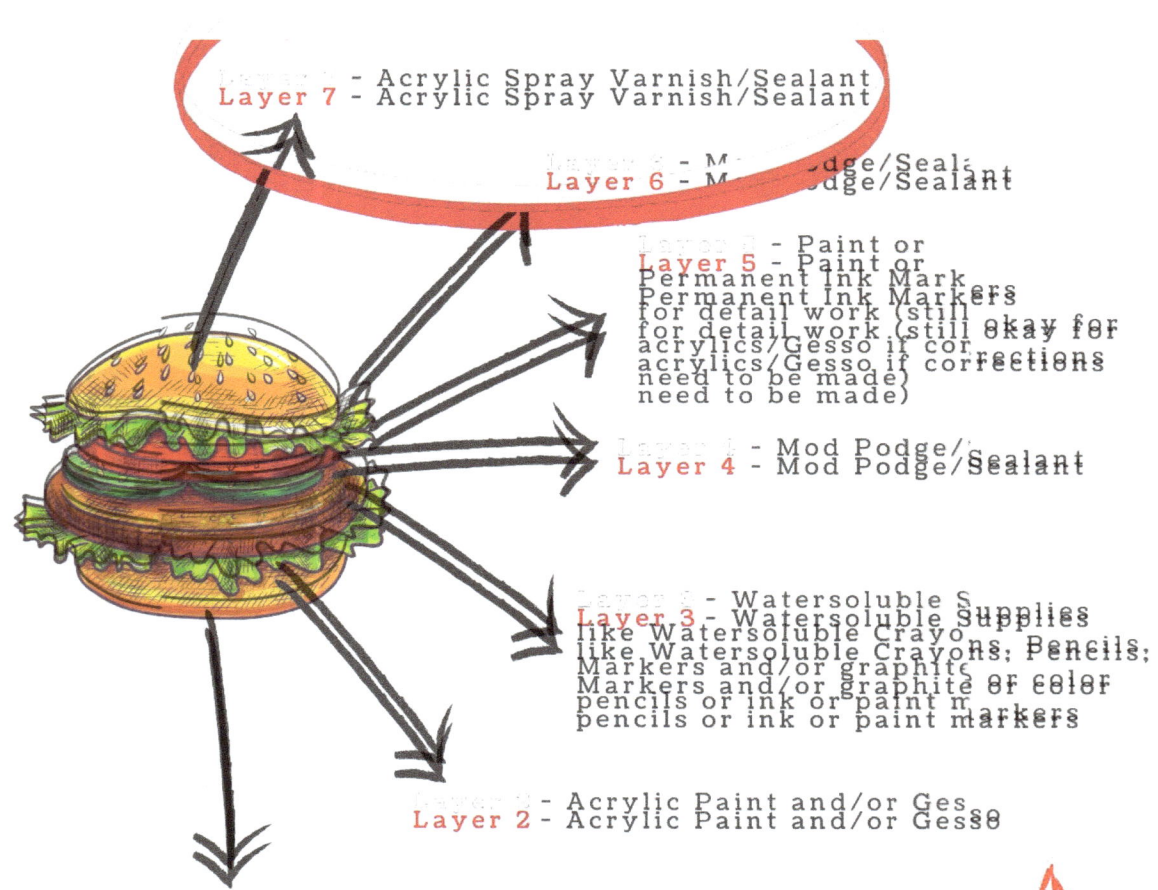

Layer 7 - Acrylic Spray Varnish/Sealant

Layer 6 - Mod Podge/Sealant

Layer 5 - Paint or Permanent Ink Markers for detail work (still okay for acrylics/Gesso if corrections need to be made)

Layer 4 - Mod Podge/Sealant

Layer 3 - Watersoluble Supplies like Watersoluble Crayons, Pencils, Markers and/or graphite or color pencils or ink or paint markers

Layer 2 - Acrylic Paint and/or Gesso

Layer 1 - Collage and Adhesive (matte medium/gel)

Build it from the bottom up ⬆

Why the Layer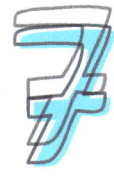

Aren't all those layers of sealants enough?

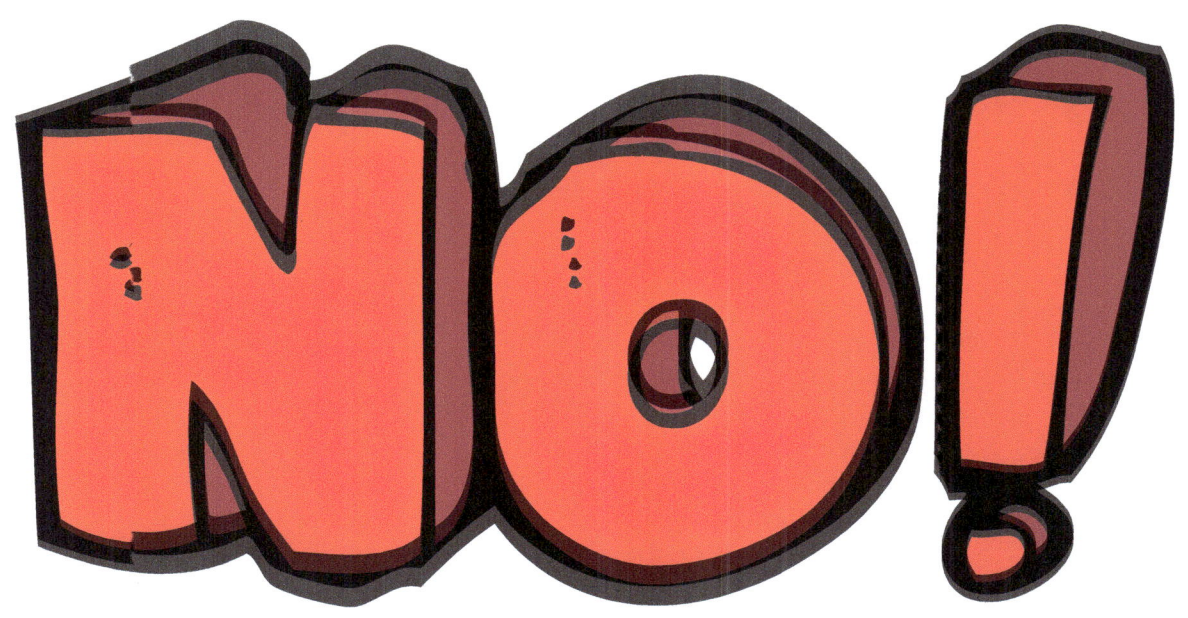

If you don't add the last layer...

❌ and you work in a journal, your pages will stick!

❌ and you hang up a canvas, dust will penetrate into it!

❌ your loved ones will be faced with a deteriorating masterpiece instead of a precious heirloom!

So please, varnish it already!

Varnish Options
Matte, gloss, spray, brush on. Clearly, you've got a choice to make!

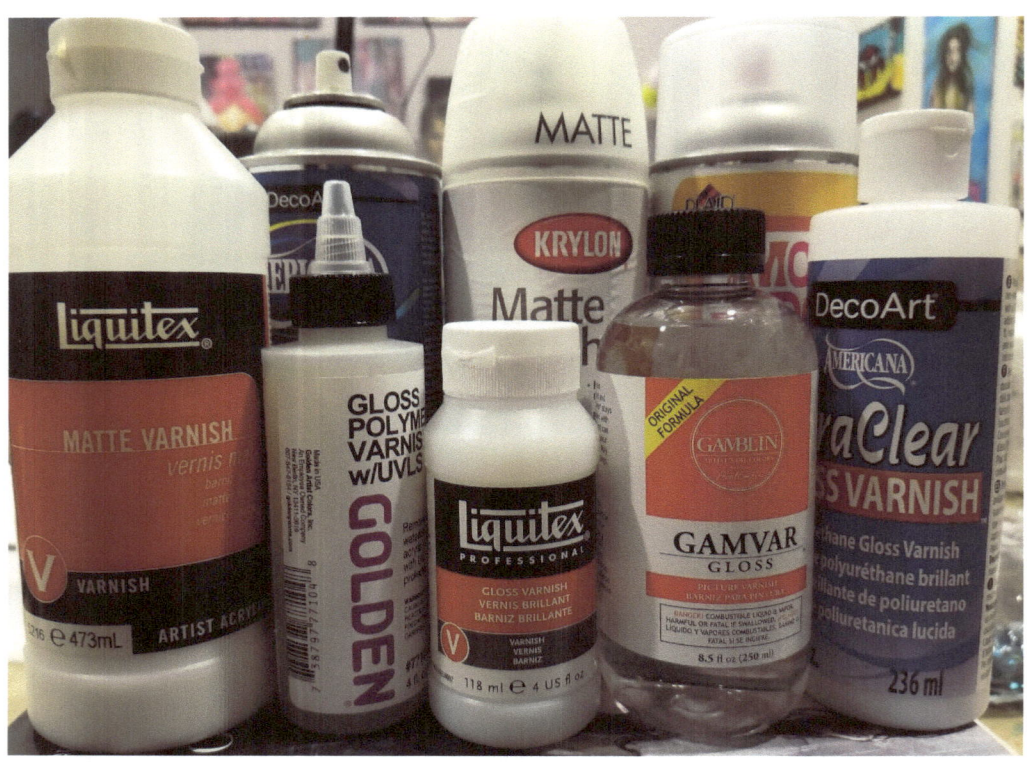

It should be noted that before varnishes are applied, it is recommended by artist professionals to apply an "Isolation Coat."

As the Golden website explains, "An isolation coat has several functions. Applied after completion of an acrylic painting, it seals the surface, lowers the absorbency of the surface, allows for a more uniform varnish application, and serves to protect the acrylic paint during varnish removal. Not applying this coat can cause serious side effects, such as the varnish absorbing into a porous support."

You can apply the Golden Brand "Isolation Coat" product or, use a sealer.

Luckily we put our last layer of Sealer on in Layer 6 so we are GOOD TO GO!

Varnish Options (Sprays)

Here is a list of the varnishes/finishes I've tried & tested.

Krylon Matte Finish Spray	**Americana Acrylic Spray Sealer**	Aleene's Spray Acrylic Sealer Matte	Mod Podge Spray Sealer Matte	
✓	✓	✓	✓	Strong Odor
✓	✓	✓	✓	Fast Drying (minutes)
✗	✗	✗	✗	UV Protect

But remember, by selecting artist grade, lightfast products, this becomes less important! You can also purchase products like Krylon's UV-Resistant Clear Acrylic Coating. It's good!

| ✓ | ✓ | ✗ | ✓ | Keeps journal pages from getting sticky |

I know for a fact that there are dozens of fabulous finishers and varnishes on the market. I apologize for not being able to list them all for you! Thankfully, you only need ONE! I'm only listing products that I personally own and have tried AND that I can recommend. I am not sponsored by these companies for listing their products here.
The spray I just happen to use most often is in bold!

Varnish Options (Brush on)

Here is a list of the varnishes/finishes I've tried & tested:

DecoArt Americana Gloss Varnish	Gamblin Gamvar Gloss	Liquitex Matte Varnish	**Liquitex Gloss Varnish**	Golden Gloss Polymer Varnish w/UVLS	
	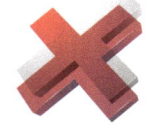	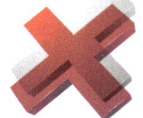	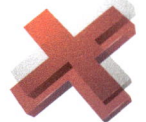		Strong Odor
	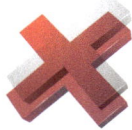			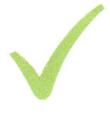	Fast Dry
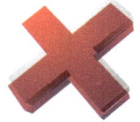	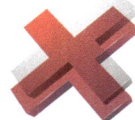			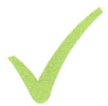	UV Protect
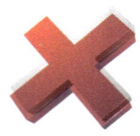		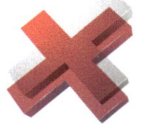	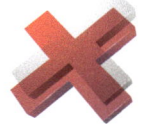		Removeable
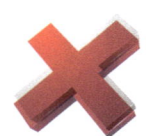	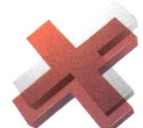	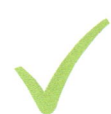	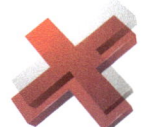	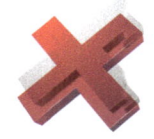	Keeps journal pages from getting sticky

As a whole, I always use an Acrylic Sealant Sprays in my art journals and I've never had a problem with my journals sticking (even with 4 coats of Mod Podge underneath). I've heard tricks like rubbing furniture wax and candle wax over journal pages but with my journals in my 120 degree attic all I can imagine are candle puddles and gooey pages.
But maybe that's just me?!
My favorite product is in bold!

Review of Layer 7

See the results "in person" as I test 8 different varnish options on canvases and art journals! psst...more on this later!

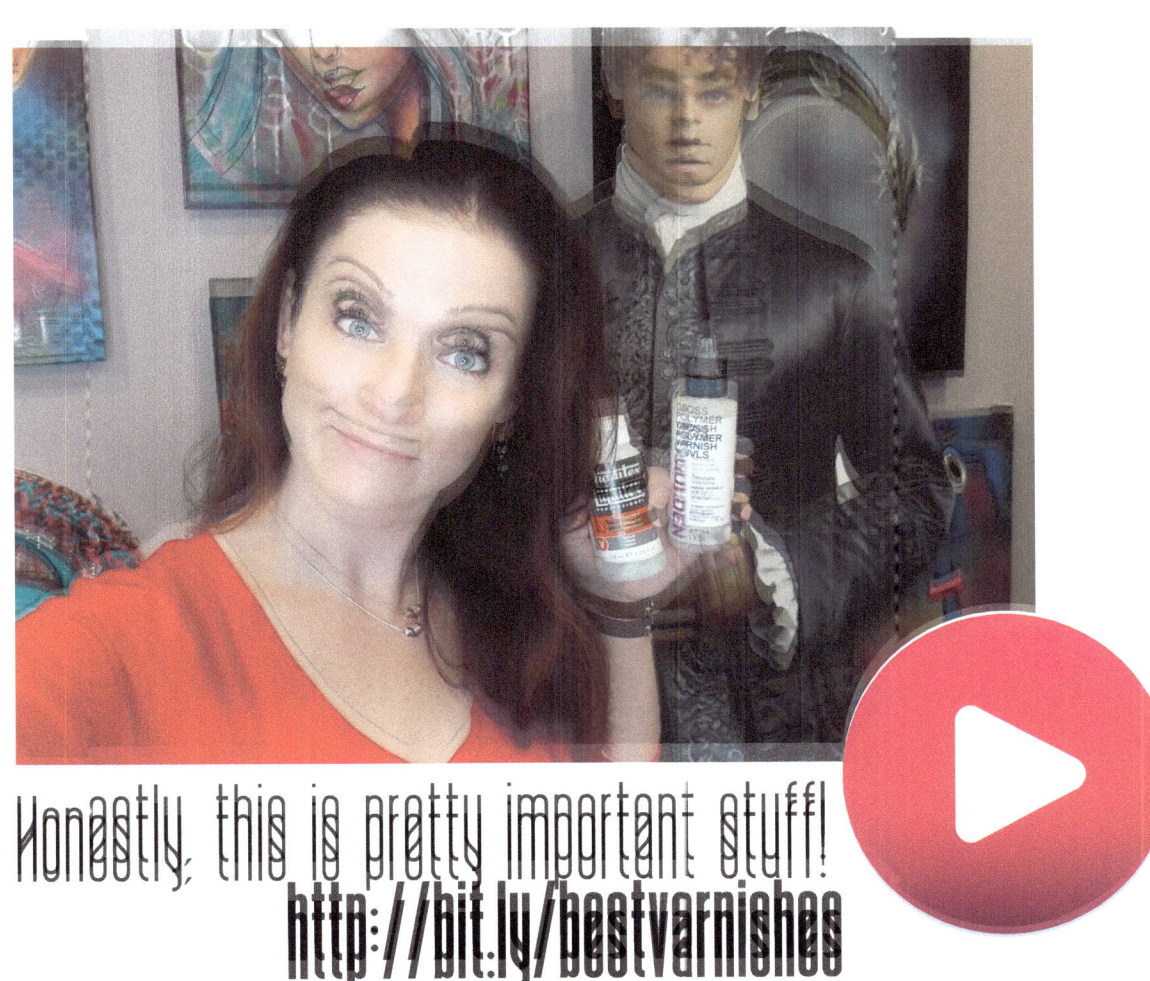

Honestly, this is pretty important stuff!
http://bit.ly/bestvarnishes

Your work of art will thank you!

Here's a recap of the whole system!

First we need a plate!

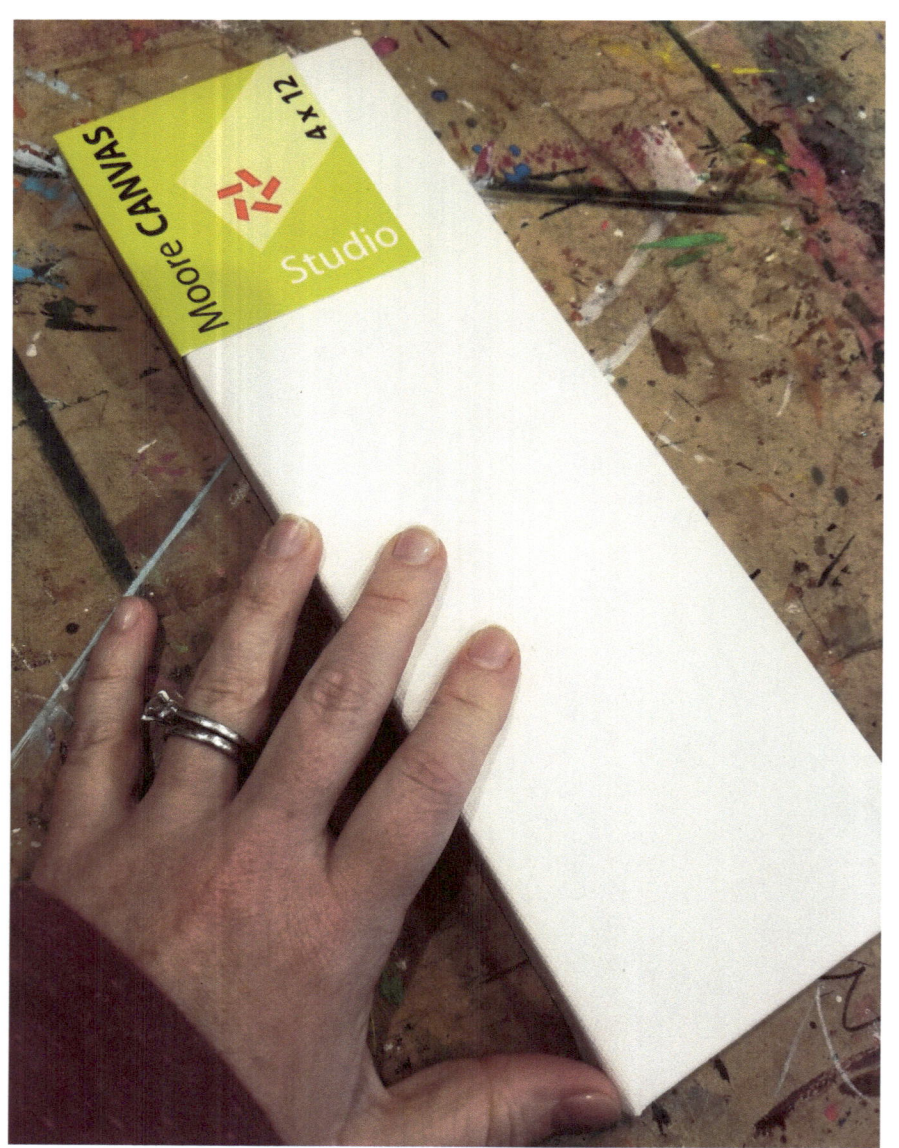

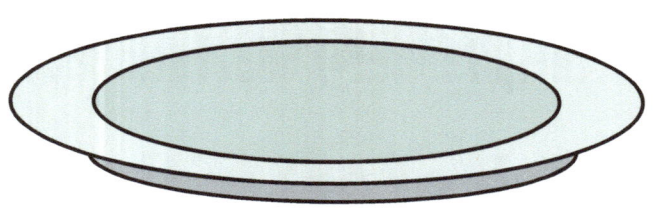

Just using 8 of these cute 4" x 12" canvases!

Then we need our Bun!

Layer  Collage it!

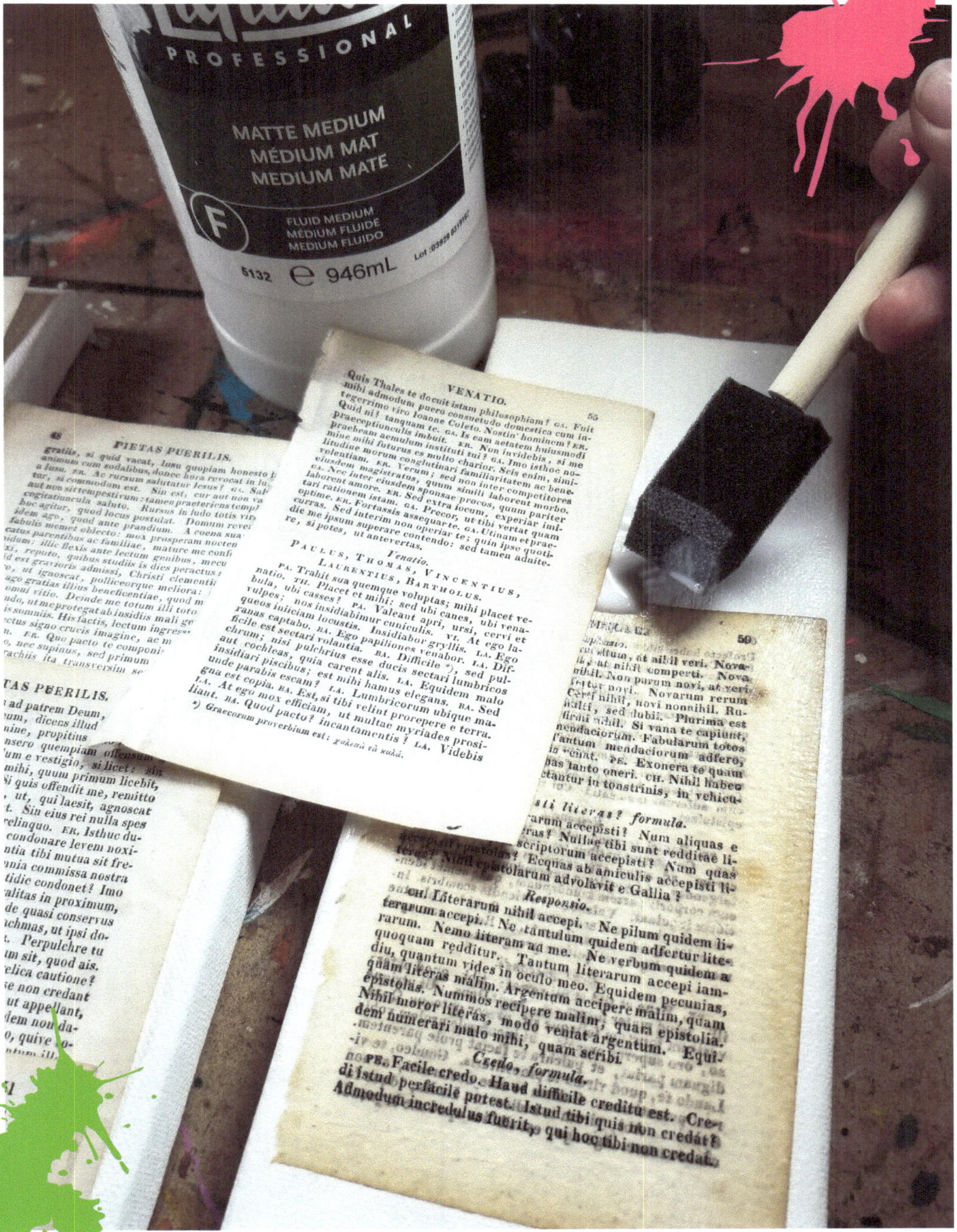

I'm using Matte Medium to glue on these vintage book pages.

When glue is dry, paint the edges!

Layer 2

Paint it!

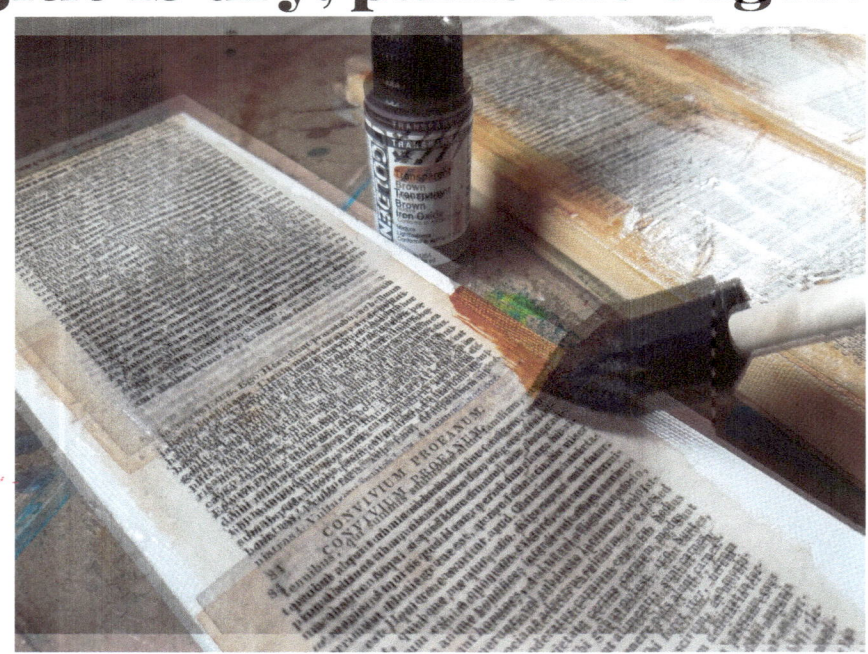

Using fluid acrylics to paint the edges.

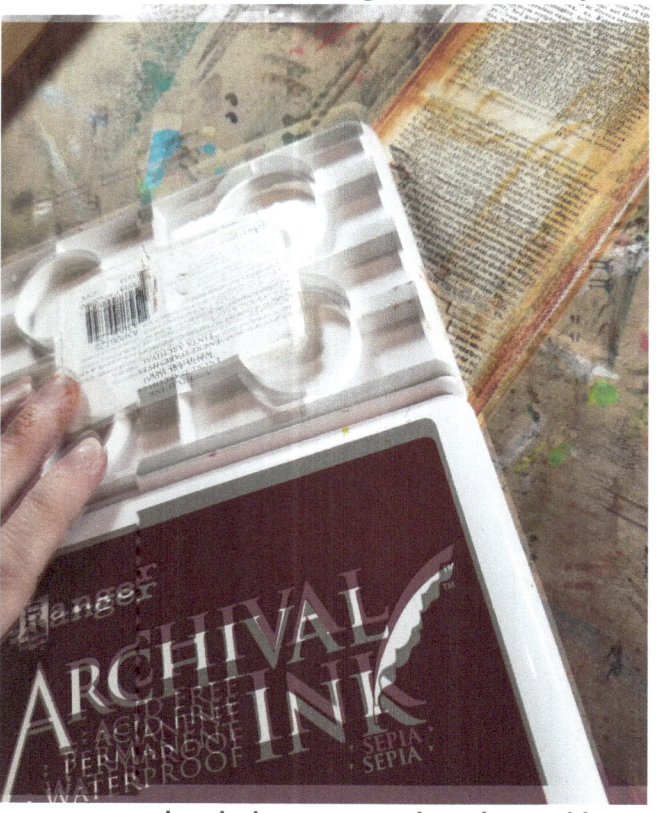

Run an ink pad around the edges to accentuate the "framed look" even further!

The sepia ink accentuates the vintage look too!

Use a hair dryer to cut drying time!
Draw your subject in the middle! Like this cool bottle!

Layer 2 Cont...

Besides faces, I love to draw bottles and vases!

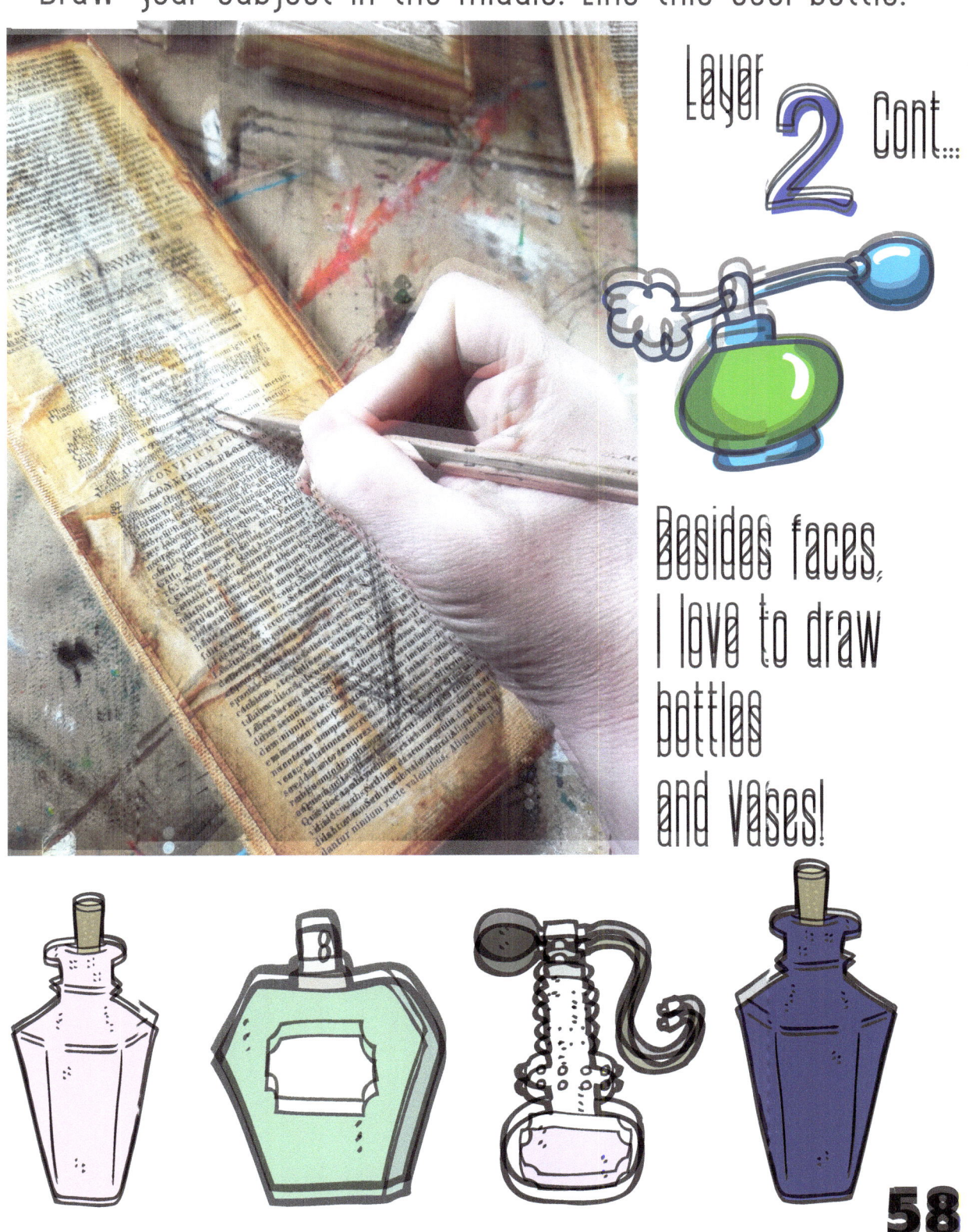

Now choose paint or ink!

Layer 2 Continued!

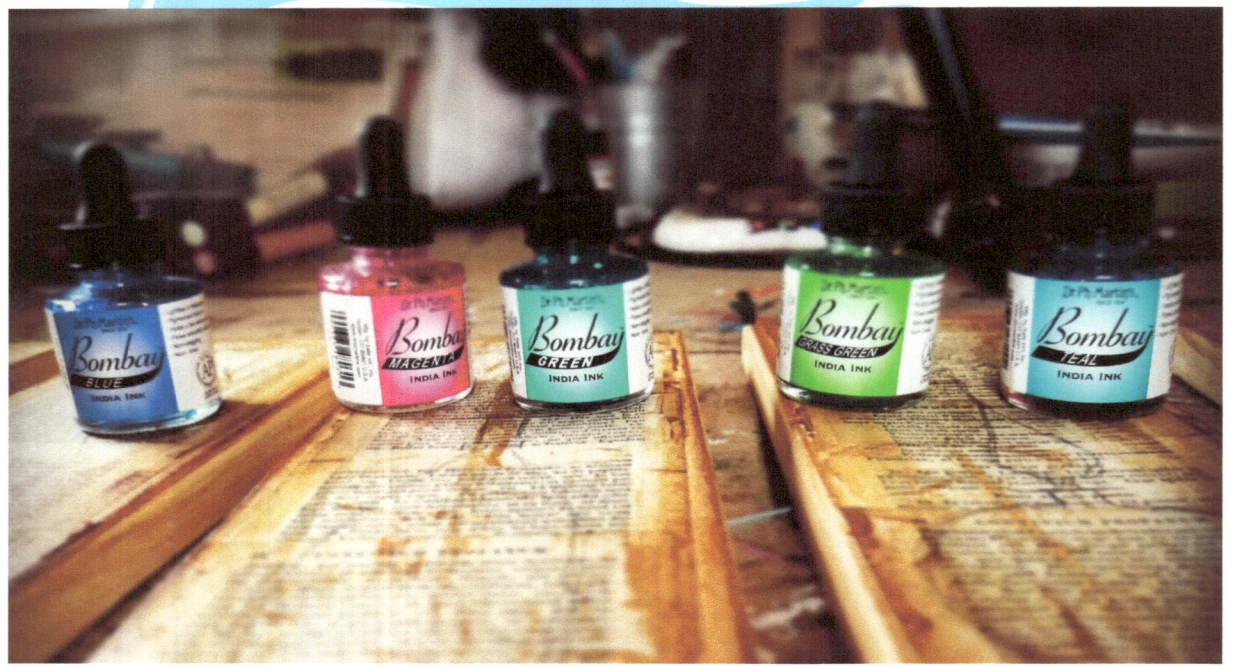

Ink is a beautiful alternative to acrylic paint. Just make sure you're using permanent ink and not watersoluble...unless you want it to ruuuuun!

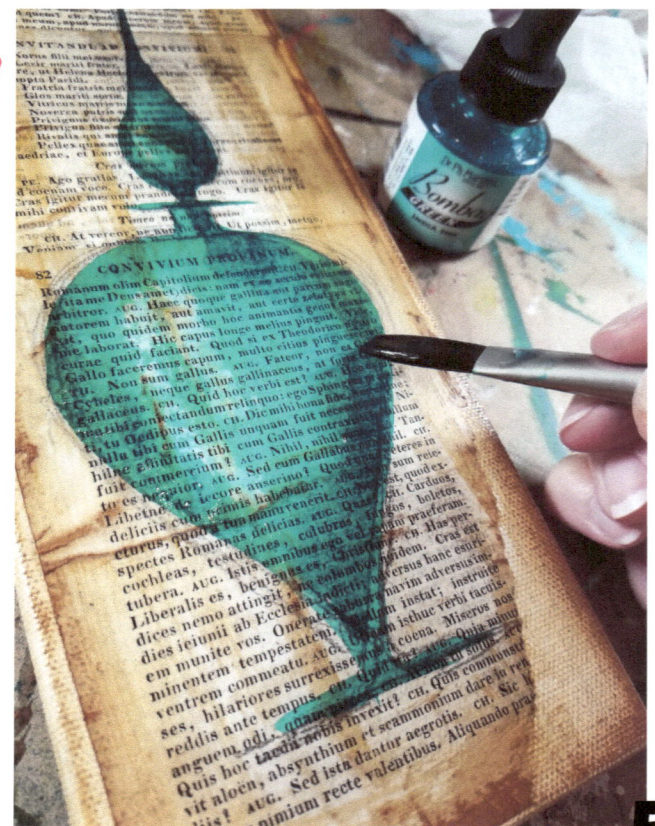

Now time for the "fun" supplies!

Layer 3 can get crazy!

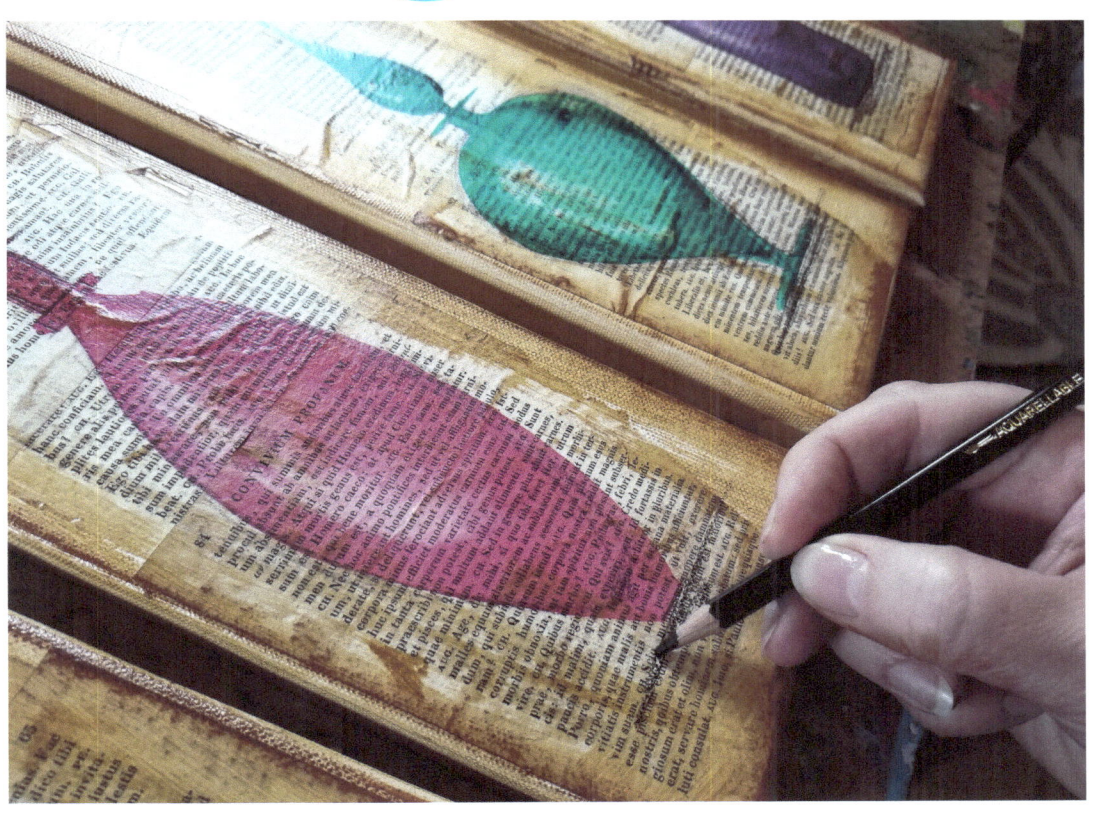

This is where you need to think of your "behavior" categories!

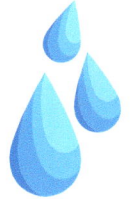      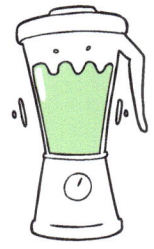   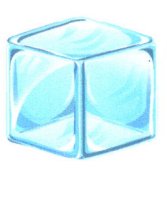

I LOVE the smeary effect that happens when my sealer in Layer 4 hits my Stabilo All pencil so I choose from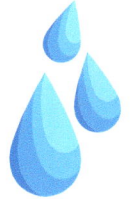

After the drawing, paint and collage...
It's time for the sealer! Yep! Layer 4

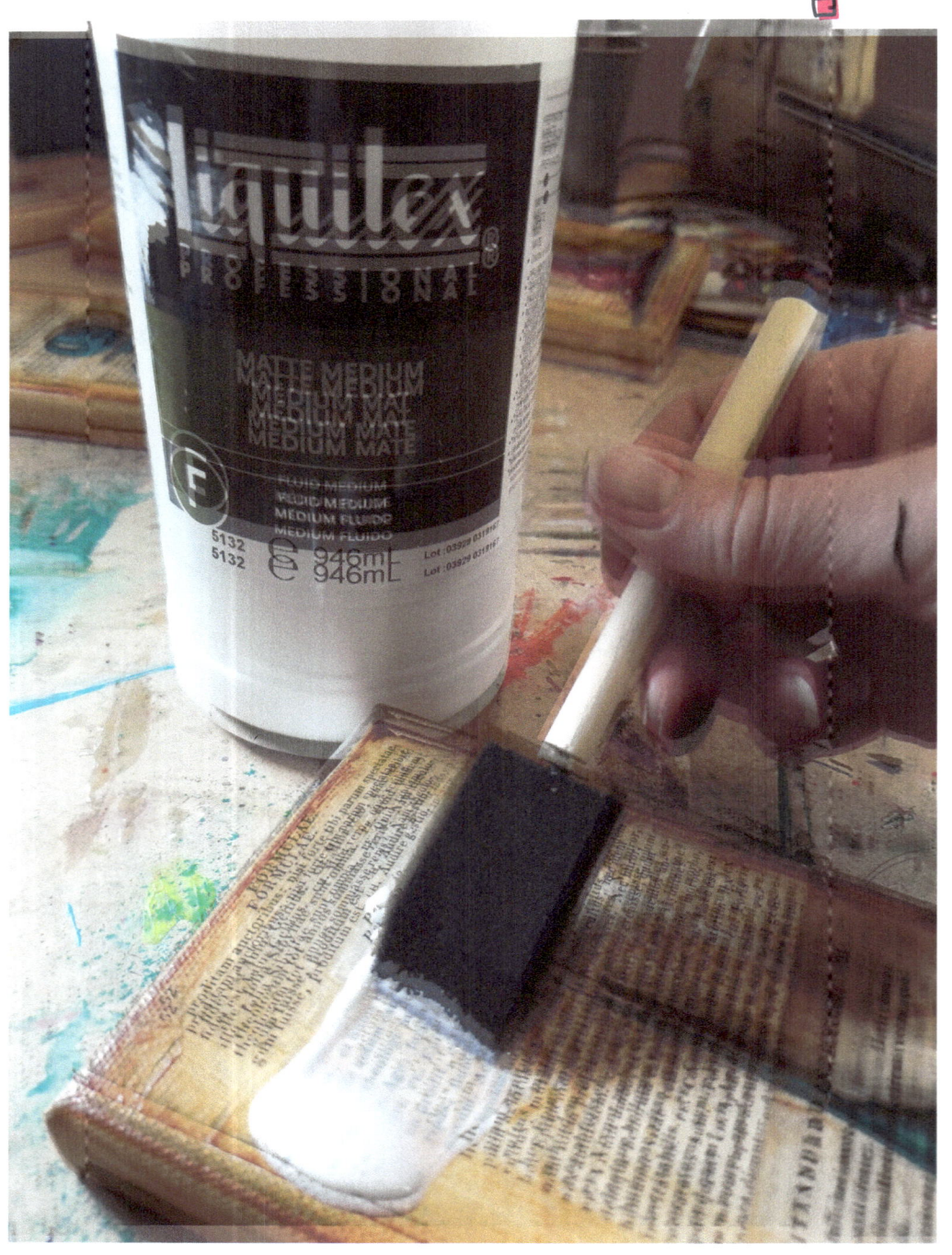

Pick your favorite sealer and smother all the layers in it!

Now it's shading time!
And just like that we're at Layer 5

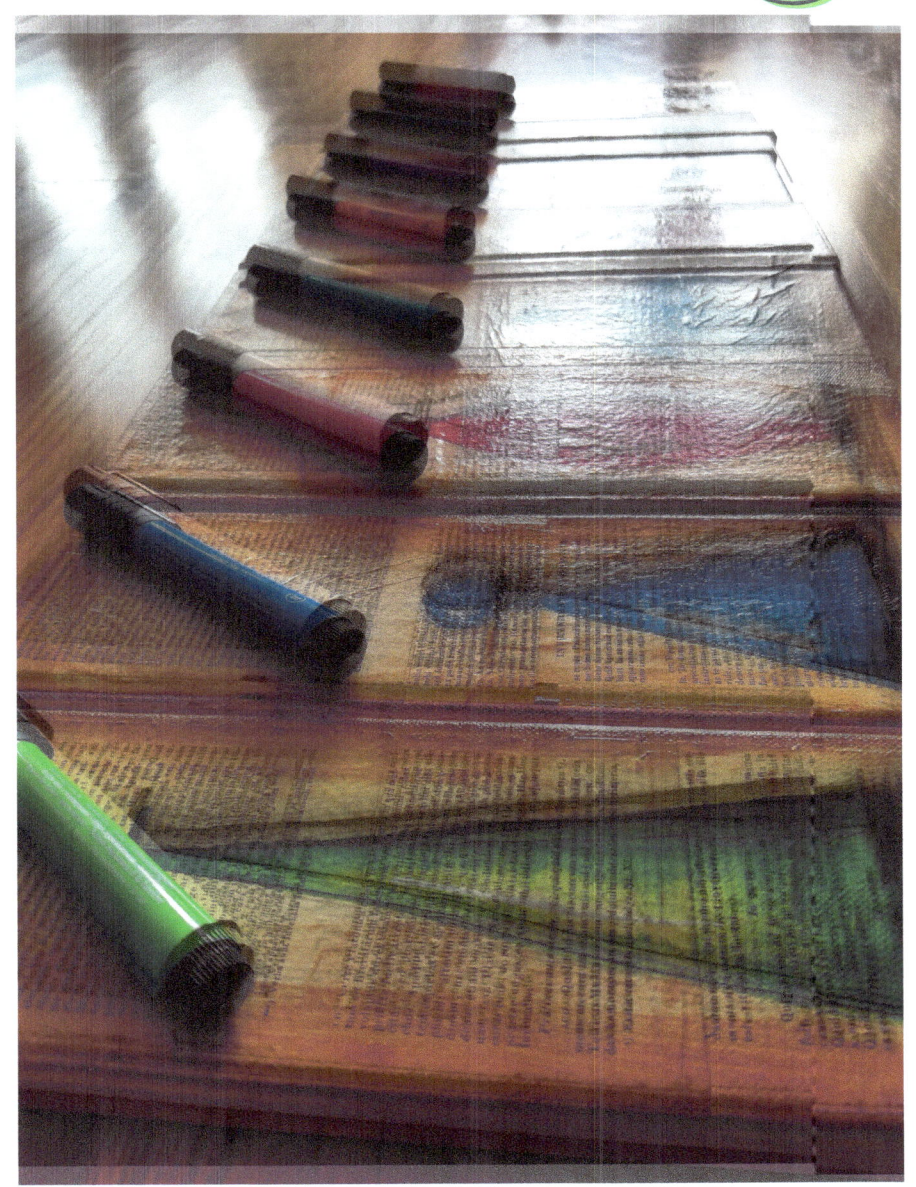

Choose a marker that matches your paint color!
I reach for Big Brush Pitt Pens every time!
You could also doodle with paint markers or just paint some more!

Where you want extra shading...

Color like a kid!!

Layer **5** continued...

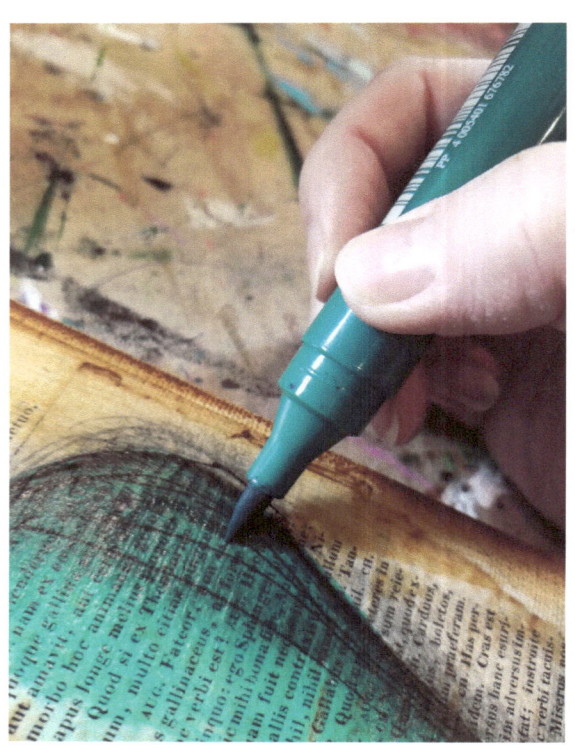

Want more dramatic shading? Then pick a darker shade from the same color family!

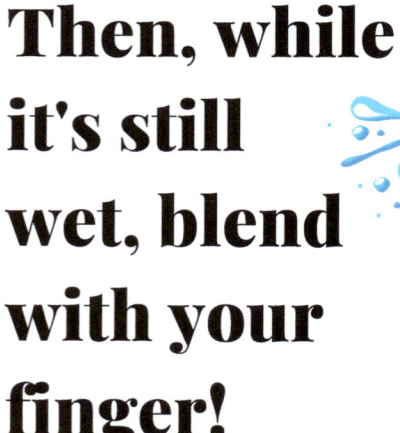

Then, while it's still wet, blend with your finger!

Don't want the blend? Then simply let it dry instead!

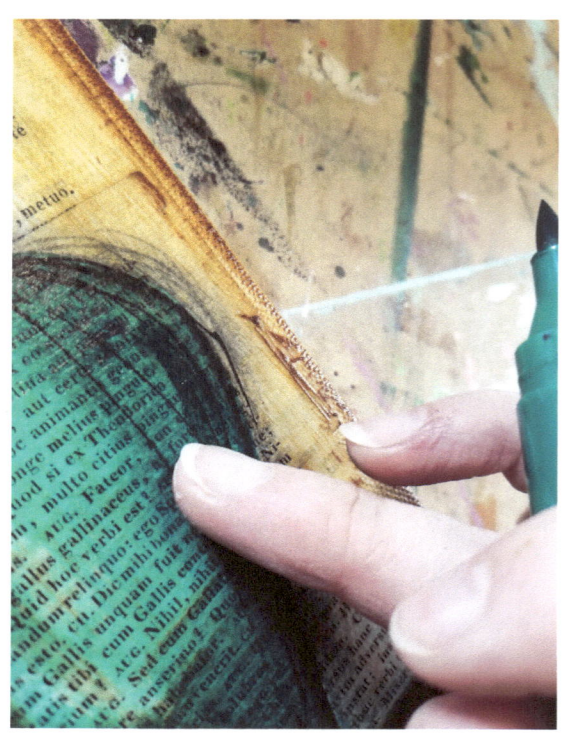

Love adding layers of depth?
You can repeat the layers over and over, as much as you like!

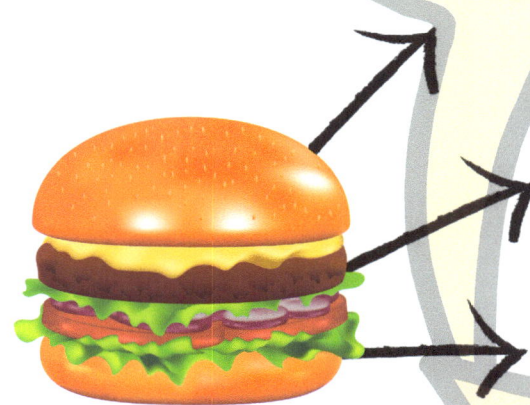

Layer 6 - Mod Podge/Sealant

Layer 5 - Paint or Permanent Ink Markers for detail work (still okay for acrylics/Gesso if corrections need to be made)

Layer 4 - Mod Podge/Sealant

Need to make a correction or go back to earlier layers?
For the most part that's no problem, you can do that too!

Just think before you apply!

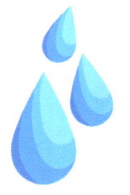  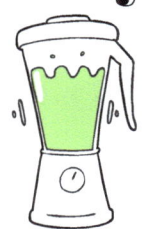 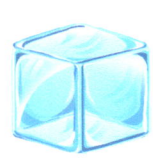

If you make a HUGE mistake...

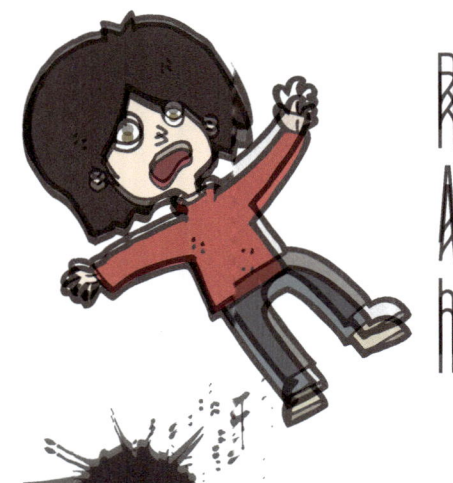

Rest assured everything will be fine!! As long as you have some Gesso to help you!

Remember, Gesso is an artist's best friend !

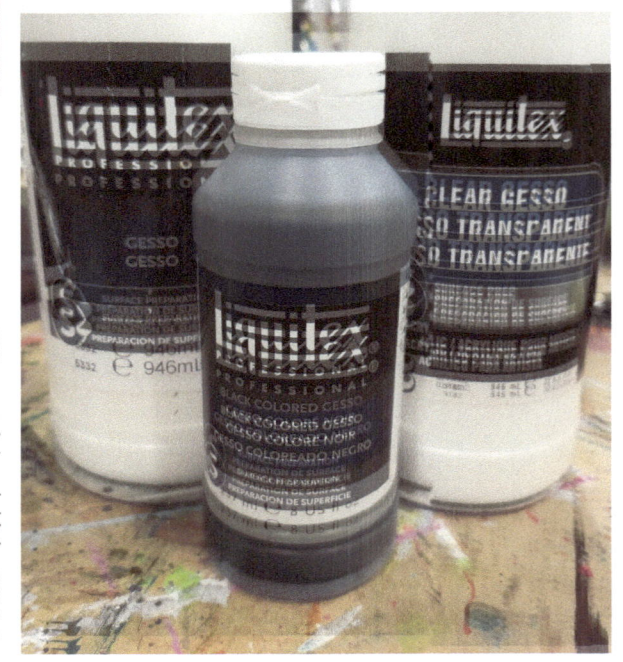

No matter what layer you make your mistake in, you can use Gesso to get you out of that mess! Make your choice of Gesso color and restart with confidence!

I use plain Gesso 90% of the time BUT I use black when I need to obliterate everything! lol!!

Seriously, relax, it's cool! It happens to the best of us!

All that's left are some final details!

Add highlights with a white paint pen! My favorite brands are Pitt Pens and Posca Pens.

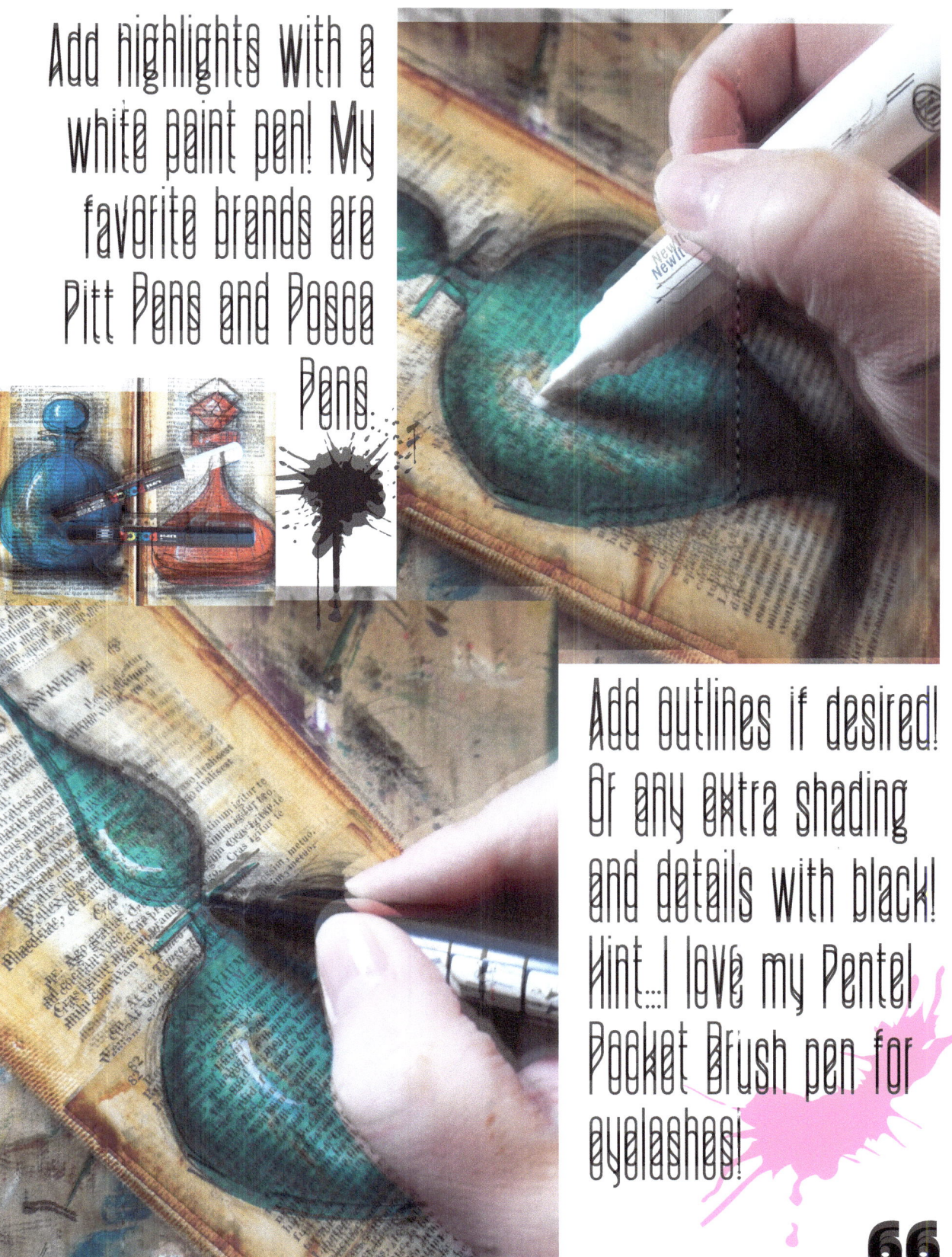

Add outlines if desired! Or any extra shading and details with black! Hint...I love my Pentel Pocket Brush pen for eyelashes!

And then all that's left to do is spray or brush on the final varnish!

Yup, we did it! All the way through to Layer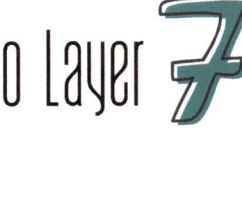

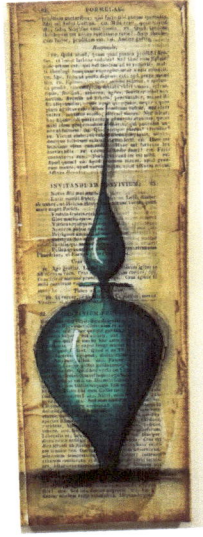

And repeat as often as your heart desires!

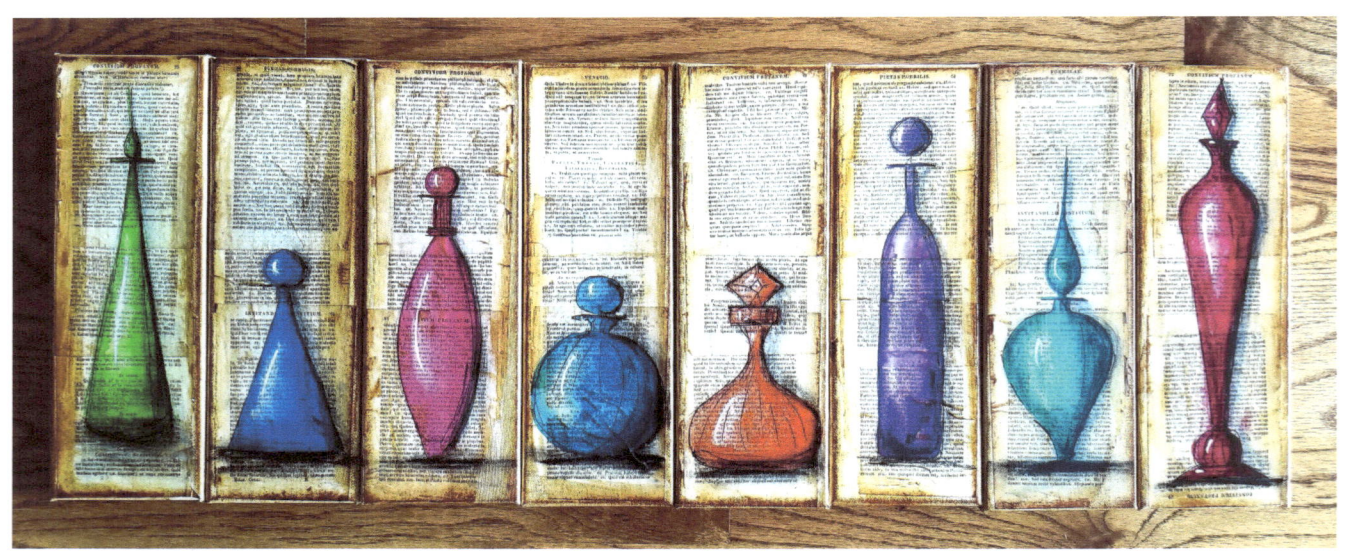

Which, evidently for me, turned out to be 8 times!

You can repeat this exact Hamburger system for any kind of subject!
Faces, animals, houses, whatever!

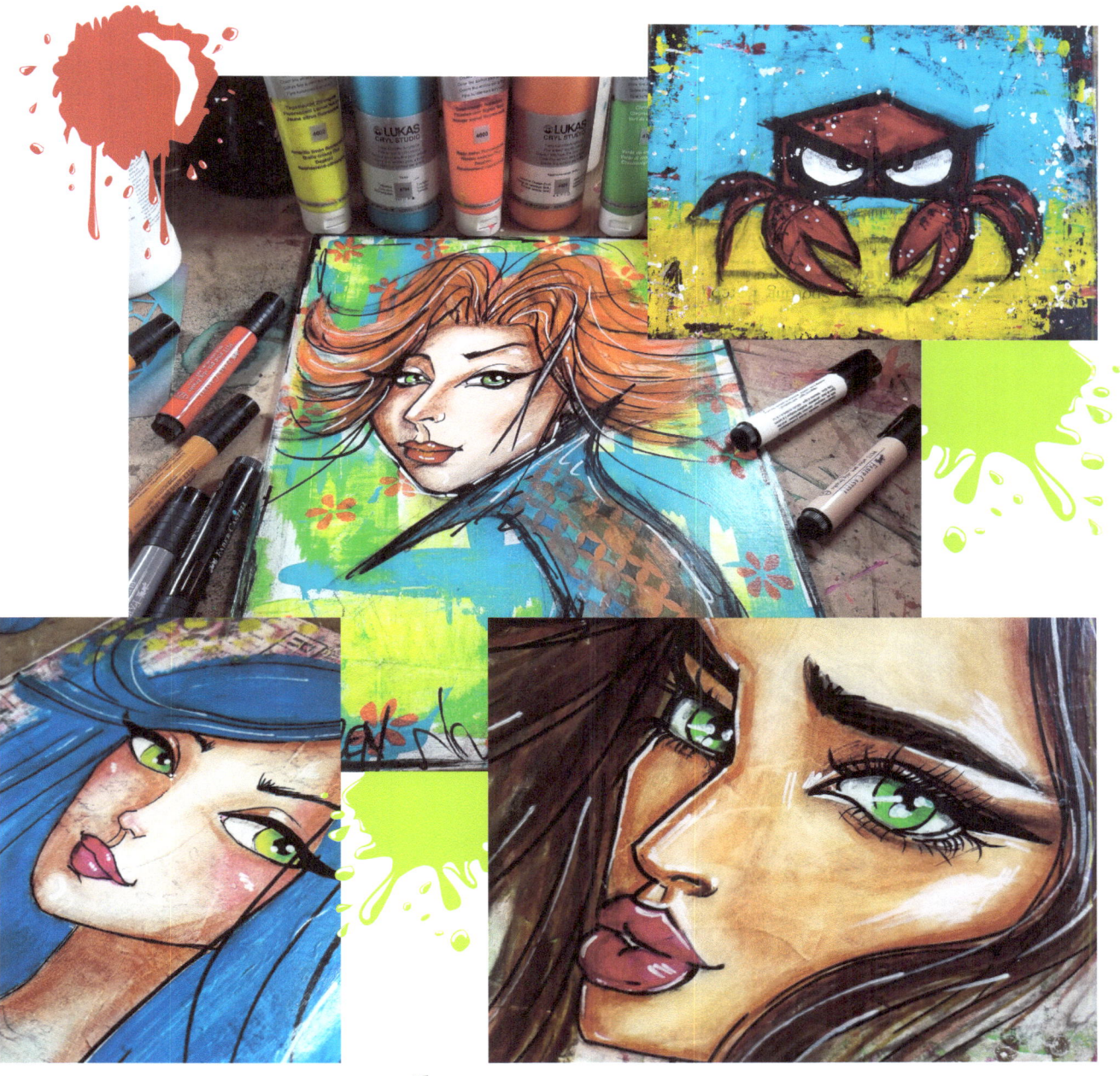

No matter what you want to create, you can trust the Hamburger System
to produce FABULOUS results!

If you want to add faces to your journal pages or need more inspiration... I got you!

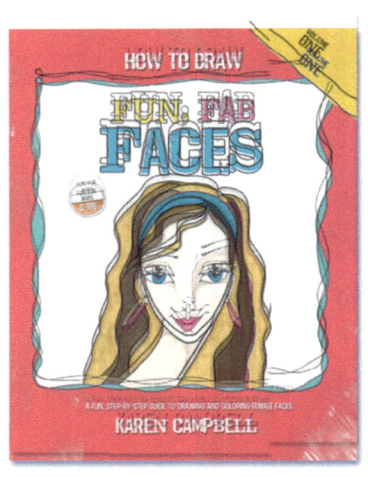
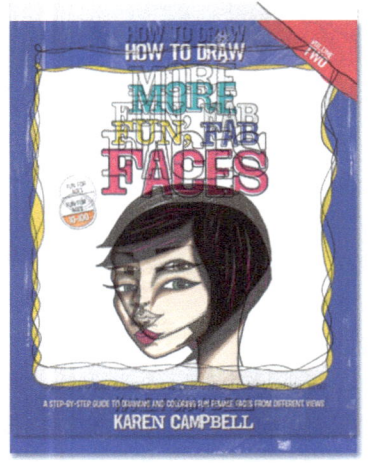
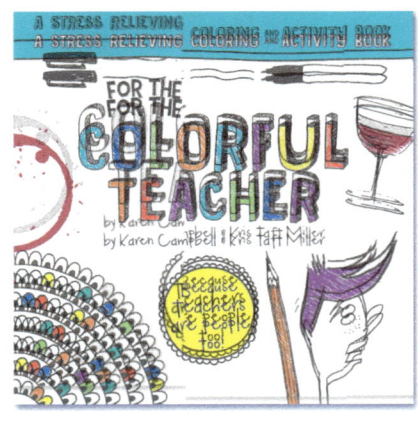
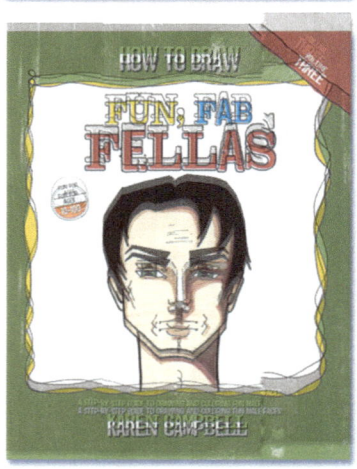
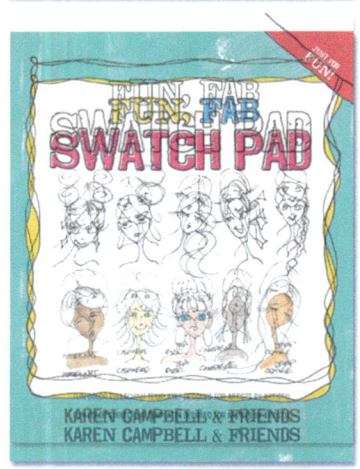
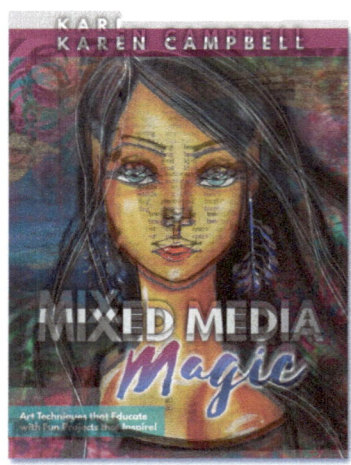
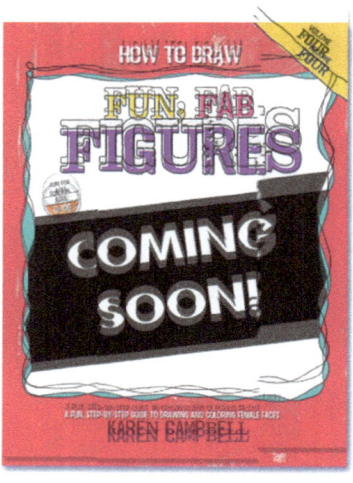
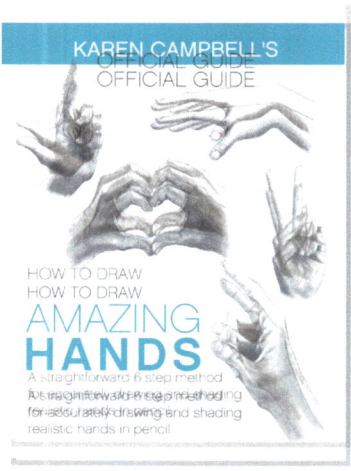
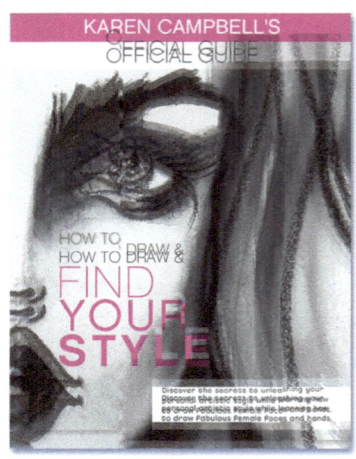

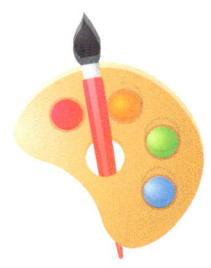

Can't get enough of mixed media fun? You would LOVE **art journaling**!

Want to learn more about Art Journaling but have NO idea where to start? This 4 part video series will give you EVERYTHING you need to get started with art journaling today! Need confidence? Ways to overcome your fear of the blank page? Looking for easy background ideas? Color choice help? Easy projects, art journal cover ideas and help covering over pages and projects you hate?? I cover all that and more! Just click the link and ENJOY!

http://bit.ly/journalwithkaren (still free!)

Let's get social...

 karencampbellartist.com

 youtube.com/karencampbellartist

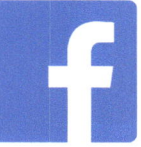 facebook.com/karencampbellartist

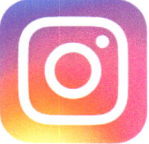 instagram.com/karencampbellartist

 pinterest.com/karencampbellartist

amazon.com/author/karencampbell

etsy.com/shop/karencampbellartist

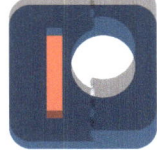 patreon.com/karencampbellartist

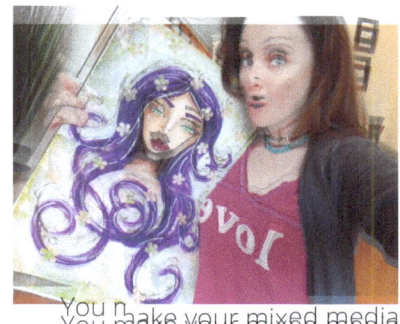

You make your mixed media projects...but in a book!

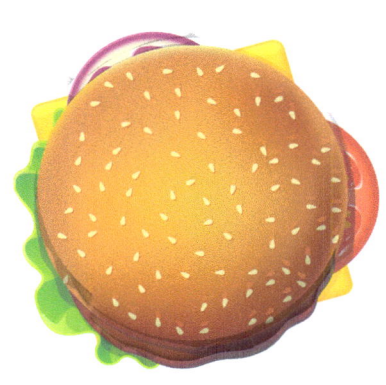

www.ingramcontent.com/pod-product-compliance
Lightning Source LLC
Chambersburg PA
CBHW051917210526
45473CB00006B/2051